BUSINESS HEAD, SPIRITUAL HEART

BUSINESS HEAD SPIRITUAL HEART

Align Your Head & Heart To Improve Performance, Profit and Happiness

SHILPA UNALKAT

First Published In Great Britain 2006
by Staflow Publishing

2nd Edition Published In Great Britain 2009
by www.LeanMarketingPress.com

To the highest power that I am capable of reaching, I pray that You allow only truth to manifest here and may only the highest good result for all concerned.

Praise

"Marrying your spiritual heart with your business mind is one of the most urgent imperatives of our time, opening the door to a whole new vision of success. Shilpa has done a great job of inspiring you to do just that."

Nick Williams | Founder of Heart at Work London,
Trustee Director of Alternatives & Author of 'The Work We Were Born To Do'

"A thought provoking book that brings a new sense of direction for today's heavily worked and stressed executives."

Subhash Thakrar | Senior Partner, Blackstone Franks LLP,
Board Director, London Chamber of Commerce &
Industry Member, Bank of England Small Business Panel

"Maximising corporate, financial and social success is the objective of every company today. Shilpa's experience in helping companies on this continuous journey is unique. This book can help CEOs, CFOs and other senior executives begin the journey via spiritual concepts."

Chandrakant Dhupelia | Chartered Accountant,
formerly with one of the Big Four Accountancy Firms

"In this insightful book, choc-full with spiritual wisdom, Shilpa has managed to provide a tool kit for living more successfully at work and always. I love the creative recipes and taster exercises that culminate in a path of self-discovery for all those seeking positive change on their journey. This book is a gift to anyone drowning in a stressful work dominated world who wants to integrate all aspects of their humanity even between 9 and 5pm."

Gill Fennings | Counselling For a Change, Therapist and Coach

"Shilpa got me to think about the big question: How can I bring my business into an expanded sense of my spirituality? I applied this approach to every business situation and the results were remarkable. The answers led me to greater prosperity, both materially and spiritually. My new attitude makes me feel so good inside and leaves me with a clear conscience. Thank you so much Shilpa for helping me understand true freedom."

Akash | CEO, Holistic Health Business

"I instructed Shilpa at a time when I was under immense pressure. So much was happening in my business and I felt overwhelmed by what was expected from me as a leader. Shilpa was a real ally and gave me a supportive structure for step by step goal setting. She was also my inner ear, sensing and feeding back her impressions which turned out to be invaluable in terms of costs savings to the company. She helped me hone in my own coaching skills to get the best from my staff and to find out what their needs and issues were. I have learned so much about myself in the time we worked together."

Peter | Director, Software Company

"Working with Shilpa is an upliftingly unique experience because of the quality with which she listens and the fullness of her commitment to her craft. There's a sense that she truly understands my quest for meaning in my life. She has the gift of an ancient wisdom that is refreshing in this modern world."

Clara | Intellectual Property Lawyer

"Having only had a few coaching sessions with Shilpa, I have already significantly improved my performance and attitude towards my role. I have been able to move past some tricky obstacles very quickly and addressed the real issues that I can actually do something about. I now have clarity about what works well (and what doesn't) and can concentrate on the areas that improve my results and the company's profit. Good coaching works and works quickly!"

Raj | Investment Banker

"Shilpa is a truly dynamic and go-getting Business Coach and Corporate Trainer who brings years of experience into her consultancy. Her coaching has made it possible for me to take positive control of my life and business with a supportive and enlightening style that has boosted my self-empowerment. I feel my whole life has now opened to so many more options than I could ever have dreamed of. Thank you."

Vivienne | Jewellery Designer

Acknowledgments

"Some people come into our lives
And move our soul to dance.
They awaken us to understanding
With the passing whisper
Of their wisdom…
They make our worlds more beautiful,
…leave footprints in our hearts,
and we are never, ever the same."

ANONYMOUS

First and foremost, my heartfelt appreciation goes to you, the reader for selecting this book amongst the huge choice out there. I hope it provides you with an inspiring model for integrating spirituality into your daily routine and through practice, opens up a beautiful vista for a happier, abundant life. As you pass through each stage of your working years, achieving your goals and ambitions, If my message invokes your sense of humility, integrity and humanity, then the work has been worthwhile.

This book places an emphasis on you, the individual – on your personal growth. Through your awakening, your business is touched, the business touches your community, the community touches the nation and thereby the world is illuminated.

From the deepest place in my heart, I express my love and gratitude to my parents, Suresh and Chandrika Unalkat. Thank you for giving me the gift of life and honouring and respecting my dreams. Your belief in me has made all the difference.

To my sister, Anjali Raja, for being my best friend and for giving me strange looks across crowded rooms. Her comic genius makes me almost incontinent. Thank you for showing me how important it is to 'lighten up' and keeping it real.

To my gorgeous princes, Shaan and Aryan, for teaching me about unconditional love and for opening my heart wider than I could ever imagine. You bring a sweetness in my life that soars way beyond words.

Shilpa Unalkat
London 2009

Contents

Introduction

"This is the time of a great beginning. It is time to die to who we used to be and to become instead who we are capable of being. That is the gift that awaits us now: the chance to become who we really are."

MARIANNE WILLIAMSON, SPIRITUAL AUTHOR & LECTURER

Do you sometimes dread going to work because you feel overworked and unappreciated? Stressed and exhausted? Bored and frustrated? Have you ever noticed that you are so terrified of losing your job that your relationship with your company is not that different from that of a slave to a plantation owner? Most of us identify with at least one of the above during our working lives.

We know by browsing the job pages that good ones are hard to come by and that many people would love to take our place, especially in a recession. There is no use moaning about the burnout – we are meant to be grateful we're lucky enough to be gainfully employed. We must work harder and smarter and sort out our problems on our own as independent, self-sufficient individuals. It is easy to feel isolated.

Do you sometimes feel as if you leave behind the 'real' you when you enter the workplace? Do you have two selves – a 'work' self and a 'non-work' self – that are so separate you can barely remember what one feels like when

1

you are being the other? What makes us believe we cannot be our true selves at work?

Whether you are a managing director, social worker or secretary, work takes up a huge chunk of your life, so it is worth ensuring that it is as fulfilling as possible. Many of us work in professions that never stir anything in us or express anything significant about ourselves. This book will help you identify times and places when you are in the 'flow' or the 'zone' and teach you how to bring that resource into the workplace with you every day. 'Flow' is the deep peace and connectivity we feel when we are enjoying living in the moment.

It is a state of total immersion in an activity, of working hard just for the sheer joy of the work. It is a common experience of peak performers. Through my executive coaching practice, I have helped countless people to bring this heightened awareness into their everyday lives. This book is a distillation of these experiences.

It is about awakening our spirit at work and creating a culture that celebrates the unity of the intellect and the heart. For our work demands our heads *and* our hearts. They are partners, not adversaries. Our aim is to have the best of both worlds – the business head for its logical brilliance and the spiritual heart for its intuitive wisdom. Through this powerful union, we can create a balanced, fulfilling and caring work environment – an environment in which all have the chance to thrive.

We live in what some might call materialistic, prove-yourself times. We admire the fastest growing companies. Finance journals list the national economies that are growing the fastest. Bigger is better and bigger-faster is better still.

Through the media we often receive the message that attending to the yearning of our soul is not going to buy us the high-flying lifestyle we should be striving for. And yet there are signs everywhere that a shift is happening. The time has come to be honest with ourselves and ask what is not really working for us anymore.

There is another kind of growth, which is much harder to measure. It is not so sought after or as admired as profitability is. It doesn't involve acquisition or skills. It is growth by a spiritual maturity. We are now ripe for this development. We have wandered for what has seemed a frustratingly long time. A sea change can only happen when the water is adequately agitated for that to happen.

Radical change has shown up our doorstep with a remarkable new persona on the world stage. The most powerful man in the world has his roots in the mud hutted villages of Kenya where no white man had ever set foot. Barack Obama's audacity to hope led him to the White House as he made history as the first black US President. What many considered as the politically impossible has now become real. Anything is possible – even moving the entire world forward to a better place. For me, President Obama is a role model that we so badly needed in our success-orientated society as he is not the stereotypical natural-born winner who rose to the top without a setback. Such people are easy to idealise, but they have little to teach us.

Visionary and humanitarian leaders are emerging in all fields of human endeavour, leading a not so quiet revolution to make a difference to the quality of life for everyone. I believe that a person's quest for a fulfilling vocation that

3

helps others is rich with meaning. At one level, the story of our work life is no more than one of many biographical strands that make up the fabric of our whole life. But on another level, the vocational journey is one where a sense of achievement is most intensely experienced – a reward for all those years of sacrifice, studying and passing exams. This is also where so many of us are *called* to contribute to the task of doing the world's work.

The business climate is also changing. A new global reality is putting visionary leadership at a premium in the workplace. Interpersonal skills are highly prized, on a par with technical expertise. We want our leaders to connect and attune first with our feelings and personal ambitions as humans and then as workers. The astute amongst our leaders will not only recognise this shift in attitude, but also honour and embrace the inclusive spirit of this new approach.

Our corporate worlds have been dominated by an intellectual focus at the expense of the inner life and the wisdom of the heart. This disassociation from the heart causes us unhappiness and leaves us feeling powerless. There are countless Machiavellian-style business books seeking to teach us manipulative tactics for clinching success. We begin to see ourselves as warriors on a massive virtual reality crusade, all aiming for one thing – to push our way to the top of the corporate pyramid by knocking off the rest.

This book is *not* such an invitation. Besides, Machiavelli ended up a failure, and so did the Princes who followed his advice. The back-stabbing politics he prescribed caused chaos in Italy for centuries.

Today's new consciousness is seeking to redress the balance, and it is no fleeting trend. It is our chance to make a real difference to a very important part of our lives. Could we be tired of inauthentic masks, mind games and greed? Revelations of corporate fraud and misdeed have led us to question fundamental human motives, turning us back to reaffirmation of basic values. Many whistleblowers are informing on millions of pounds of financial fraud as their moral beliefs give them the courage to stand up against wrongdoings.

On a personal level, we no longer want our lives to be measured in terms of how much we produce, but in the quality of our life experiences. We are more than our salary. This book is written from the premise that without spiritual fulfilment, material success is empty. And that spiritual growth is hindered when someone is chronically worried about their material security.

Daniel Goleman coined the phrase emotional intelligence when he noticed how some people seemed to get on and become successful without being particularly intellectually bright. Emotional Intelligence is the intelligence that understands moods, body language and cultivates self-awareness and motivation. Danah Zohar formulated another concept beyond this idea – that of Spiritual Intelligence. This is a way of being that often chooses not to adapt and behave 'appropriately' and that uniquely steers away from mainstream. It is an intelligence that looks for vision and purpose and is transformative and creative. I am encouraging you to clear your mind of old and destructive thought patterns and discover new non-traditional ways of thinking! I am not alone in my quest. Spirituality is becoming a key theme within business academic research.

Introduction

Some business schools are now offering MBA courses on spirituality in the workplace.

Common sense alone leads me to believe that 'spiritual' companies are better companies because of their higher ethics. They are also much more attractive to well-rounded employees who make it their responsibility to enhance their personal development, and ultimately their contribution to the growth of the business. There will be little or no divide between their home and work lives as the values are beautifully compatible and aligned.

Think about what you truly want from your workplace and then have the courage and wisdom to do something towards making this your new reality. Use the inspirational thoughts and quotes to uplift and encourage you to start bringing about a spiritual revolution at work. Aligning what we do, who we are and what we most value transforms our workplace into a playground where our soul is nurtured.

I am not suggesting you must do all the exercises at the end of the chapters (I am an optimistic realist!). Choose those that resonate with you. All I ask is that you pay attention to what moves in you when you do any exercise and listen for the call that dares you to take positive action. The exercises are there to help you discover some insights about yourself and your work environment and you may encounter some satisfying 'aha' moments. This shift in your awareness happens at a deeper level and not only will you have a solution to a puzzle, but you will recognise it as authentic truth. You may even be aware that something permanent has happened – a transformation has occurred.

This book has been written with an open heart.
I invite you to read it with an open mind.

Part One

Realisation

The Corporate Condition:
The Talented, Disillusioned Executive

"The feeling of being hurried is usually born of a vague fear that we are wasting our life. When we do not do the one thing we ought to do, we have no time for anything else - we are the busiest people in the world."

ERIC HOFFER, AMERICAN AUTHOR

On the surface she has the life she dreamed of as an ambitious young woman. She sailed through university and law school to become a successful corporate lawyer. At the age of 30 a lucrative partnership is within sight. It is hers for the taking if she can only work a little harder. She has a corner office, her own secretary, the respect of her peers, staff who look up to her.

She owns a large apartment in a desirable part of London. Her wardrobe is full of clothes that wouldn't look out of place on the pages of *Vogue* magazine. But sadly, this is a home she rarely spends time in other than to lay down exhausted at night. And she sometimes wishes these beautiful clothes were seen by people other than colleagues, clients and the hordes of anonymous people carefully avoiding eye contact with each other on the commute to and from work.

Every morning it's the same frantic routine. An alarm rips her from her heavy slumber while it's still dark outside. In her early twenties she took it in her stride, but as time went on she noticed her body was protesting more and more. The day came when she had no choice but to place the alarm clock at the other side of the room so that the snooze button was out of reach. The dash across the room to slap the clock into silence sets her heart racing and it doesn't stop until after she is back in bed that night – usually quite a while after.

In between duty calls. She puts on a suit and a gladiator mentality, grabs her briefcase and makes a run for the tube station. Breakfast is a coffee and a croissant consumed with the same frantic urgency that characterises all her movements. By 8.00 am she is in work and there she will remain until that time in the evening, assuming it's not a particularly busy day. Twelve hours later, when she closes her computer down and picks up her briefcase, she desires nothing more than a warm bed, or bath, or embrace. But instead of following her instinct to hurry home, most nights she finds herself carried, as if on automatic pilot, to the smoky, crowded bar round the corner from the office.

It is an unspoken rule that anyone who wants to get ahead in the firm must spend at least three nights a week in here, back-slapping with 'the team'. Those who are really serious about success will be there four or five nights. A few glasses of Burgundy have the same effect as a valium pill. At least she can get to sleep on these nights. When she has not had her 'medication' she sometimes tosses and turns for hours, the minutiae of current law cases running through her head.

This young woman has success, status and money but what about peace of mind, joy and fulfilment? In the early days of her career she did not even notice she was sacrificing the latter three. After the carefree days of university she was hungry for a challenge, ready to throw herself into a career. But over time the buzz of the adrenalin rush has become deafening. Her mind too preoccupied to see her situation clearly, her body speaks to her in aches and pains and an almost constantly upset stomach.

She notices there are a few times when the physical discomfort goes away and her mind, too, is at ease. Hanging out with friends on a Saturday, preparing food and chatting away. On Thursday nights, sitting on a yoga mat chanting with other class members. On rare holidays or weekends away when walking through a majestic forest or horse riding on a Somerset beach. Anytime she watches her one-year old nephew greeting the world with wide-eyed amazement and playful love.

These are all windows into another dimension, and they open up a yearning within her. She tries to silence it by reminding herself that as nice as these experiences are, there is 'reality' to consider. There is work to be done, money to be earned, a mortgage to be paid, achievements to be notched up. Those special moments are very nice, but it's not as if we can feel peaceful, joyful and fulfilled all the time, she rationalises. Or can we?

That successful but unhappy young lawyer was me.
And this book is the answer to my question.

SACRIFICING YOUR LIFE - FOR WHAT?

Tom Peters, who wrote the book, *In Search of Excellence*, said that excellence is a high-cost item and you must give up things to achieve it. He was referring mainly to professional and material excellence and he said that what you must give up is *"family vacations, Little League games, birthday dinners, weekends, lunch hours, gardening, reading, movies, and most other pastimes."* In other words, the very things that make up our fondest memories; the activities that make life enjoyable, keep us out of the divorce courts and away from the doctor, and make life beautiful, balanced and graceful. It seems to suggest that all work and no play make you a valued employee.

My doctor once advised that one should never get so immersed in work that you give up other goals or responsibilities. No matter how satisfying our work, it cannot make our lives complete. You may miss out on the rich opportunities of a multi-faceted life. One of my clients, a pensions actuary, said that the best investment for him was taking six months out and spending quality time with his family. A Balanced life portfolio is key to a rich life. In the current recession many people are naturally fretting that if they lose their jobs, then this will take away from them the principal way in which they fulfil and manifest their essence in this world. Those are about to lose their work, or who have lost it, fret because deep down, subconsciously, they believe that work is the only way in which they can fulfil who they were meant to be. There are so many other mediums by which this can be achieved whether through the love of your family, friends, interests or helping out at a charity. You are much more than your job.

Was what Peters called 'excellence' just another word for workaholism? The Japanese language has a word for 'death by overwork' – karoshi. You don't get a word like that in your language unless there are a few statistics to back it up! Workaholism, which broadly speaking is simply the compulsion towards busyness, has all the characteristics of an addiction. The worker becomes so preoccupied that it distorts their experience of time. They become compulsive and talk about work all the time, even if they bore the pants off everyone else. Often it has almost an 'anaesthetic' effect, covering painful issues in their personal life. You hear of people who lock themselves away in their offices and this cocoon comfort zone becomes a substitute for any sort of meaningful relationship. Their family are often quite upset by this and arguments flare up at home. When this becomes more serious, the person cannot function without this 'drug' and even hobbies or taking a holiday gives them withdrawal symptoms. Do you recognise these characteristics in yourself or anyone you know?

What sets workaholism apart from other addictions is that it is socially accepted. We don't bat an eyelid when someone says they are so busy with work they can't take a holiday this year – it seems almost impressive and indicates that the person is a hard working, productive member of society. Let's face it, it looks good and work is often used as an excuse to avoid certain situations or events.

Yet I have noticed that effective workers do what is necessary to finish a project and then relax, whilst work addicts can't seem to stop checking and re-checking. It's never quite right and they seem to create more work for themselves. As an employer you may think this is great and will increase productivity, but a workaholic environment creates burn-out quickly. Taken too far, many health and psychological problems stem from what could be described as a narrow-minded, addictive mindset that dominates our work environment. The term 'Type-A personality' was coined by heart specialists Meyer Friedman and Ray Rosenham to describe individuals who are competitive and hard driving. Not surprisingly they found that Type-A people are three times more likely to have a stroke or heart attack than Type-B people who take life more calmly.

It is no coincidence that the American Medical Association discovered some years back that the majority of heart attacks happen at around nine o'clock on Monday mornings. This undoubtedly has something to do with what most of us are doing around this time, which is going back to work. Or more precisely, going back to work we don't like, work that doesn't match our spiritual core, and work that can literally break your heart.

It is indicative of the society we live in, that the unhealthy drive and ambition exhibited by Type-A people is actually welcomed and encouraged in the corporate world. It can hardly then come as a surprise that many Type-B people may feel pressurised to emulate these patterns of behaviour to be counted in for promotion. In my opinion the Type-A personality is an unhealthy mental make-up. Underneath it there is always a voice, whether it is a whisper or shout, which tells us there is a better way. Over time this gets louder and louder and the end result could be a breakdown, burnout or even worse, a heart attack.

AWAKENING YOUR SOUL AT WORK

A central premise of the ancient Bhagavad-Gita is that a wise person performs work for the joy of the work itself, without attachment to results or rewards. In this way, one surmounts the ego and grows in wisdom and awareness. Letting go of the need to control the outcome and instead serving the unfolding reality is extremely potent. Nelson Mandela spent 27 years in prison, focussed on his intent to create a post-apartheid era in South Africa. He could have dwelled on how unlikely it was that he would ever get out of prison. It must have been increasingly difficult as the years passed on for him to hold steadfast to his dream instead of panicking or despairing. Because he was true to his work, he emerged from prison with tremendous strength and power to inspire the world when finally the time came for the country to transform.

If I have learned anything from my own journey, it's to look beyond life's window dressing. I've grown more tolerant and finally understood that wholeness is really the goal. It has helped me counterbalance society's overemphasis on worldly success and I'm better at dis-identifying from the results of the efforts I have made. To do one's best and then to let outcomes be what they will is to acknowledge realistically how often they are beyond our control and to guard against neurotic attempts at controlling how things turn out. You know the behaviour – everything from dishonesty to defensiveness.

Notice how when you give one hundred percent, you are happier and more enthusiastic. If a thing is worth doing, it is worth doing willingly. This is how you increase your vitality and generate fresh energy. These are the days when you have momentum and get things done on your checklist. When you work willingly you attract a greater flow of cosmic energy into the body and will hardly ever be tired. Remember how that felt – when you rolled up those sleeves, worked hard yet you weren't drained but found it satisfying? Swami Paramahansa Yogandanda, saint and philosopher – a rare genius who taught the secrets of spiritual existence describes this wonderfully: *"When I am with people, I am with them wholly, with the greatest joy; and when I am alone, I am alone with that joy. When I work, I work with the greatest will and happiness. No matter what your task, do it joyously and willingly. If you don't you will only devitalize yourself. And remember to always be sincere. Through sincerity you can work more harmoniously with others."* (The Divine Romance p.188)

Whenever I get a cab, I often notice that some taxi drivers make my trip so pleasant with their cheerfulness, whilst others who are miserable make it a real pain and I just can't wait to get out! The ones who are friendly and relaxed are that way because they are giving a great service. When you are only thinking of the money and give only fifty percent effort, you suffer much more than your employer. He only loses a few pounds – you lose your self-respect and a whole chunk of your life. Giving your best will really help you to enjoy your work.

It is salutary to note that the word 'success' originally had nothing to do with 'good' results, much less with the accumulation of wealth. It meant simply *whatever follows after something*. It's a neutral word. Quite relaxed and easier on us. Much nicer than the self-aggrandisement that passes today for living 'successfully'!

Spend time with a two year old and you will soon hear the words "No!" and "Mine!" These are the cries of the ego which is just developing in the toddler. The ego tries to secure power by imposing its will. Success does not have to involve negative tension. Do we really need to be frantic, aggressive and struggling all the time? The ambitious tension can keep us in a state of contraction. Trying to take centre stage in meetings to impress others, using uncontrolled 'bullish' foul language or caustic sarcasm without any thought to how it affects others. Bravado is often a cover up for a lack of real expertise. This posturing behaviour seems to give us energy, but doesn't really. It is akin to the immediate and short high we feel when we down an espresso shot. If you are involved in a conflict ask yourself is it worth the struggle. Is it important? Does it have value? Will the outcome serve you or others? Often we are tempted to hold onto our position, especially if we have invested time and energy into it.

Imagine how the workplace would look if you softened your eyes. Maybe the gruff receptionist would seem kinder? It takes a surrendering and letting go for the softness to make its way into our hearts. We all know some people to whom this would be anathema, because any easing up feels like defeat. Yet if we take the time to stop and realise that this is a form of mastery, of actually taking positive control over our response we can then begin to feel what a relief this approach is. It frees us and it frees others around us. Being considerate and mindful of our words is far from weak – it reveals a poised, self-confident character. This is especially hard to do in a culture as in the UK that applauds, almost smirks at clever expressions of cynicism. Snide comments revel in their ability to expose the 'truth' about how all of our heroes are actually fools and there is nothing to believe in. How long before President Obama too falls victim to this national pastime?

A paradox is something that appears contradictory and yet it is true. We 'control' by letting go – we 'win' by surrendering. We can even move forward by standing still. When we most want to force our will on someone that is when we should release. When we most want to have our own way that is when we should sacrifice. The irony is that by making these contradictory moves, we find what we are looking for.

One of my clients was a managing director in his mid-fifties. I'll call him Alan. Before coming to see me he was a high achiever who had climbed up the corporate ladder for over 30 years of career dedication and life sacrifice. He worked 12-hour days, travelled abroad at least two weeks out of every month, and had long been a near stranger to his wife and three children.

By the time he came to see me he had received a wake-up call. A routine medical check showed that his blood pressure was dangerously high. He was put on a very high dose of medication and warned that he needed to make some big changes in his lifestyle. At first he had protested, he told me, saying that it was the norm in his industry and there was nothing he could do about it. His doctor's response had been blunt: "And how many of your peers have died of a heart attack before the age of 60?"

This was the first time he had ever been forced to question the way he was living his life. It was the first time he had considered that he had choices about how to spend his time and energy; until then he had never stopped for long enough to reflect on the life decisions he was making, and whether there were better ones available to him.

We started off by getting clear about what his objectives in life were, so that we could then consider his options. He realised for the first time that he had been addicted to the adrenalin buzz his high-stress lifestyle brought him, but that it had never given him the depth of fulfilment he wanted. He also realised that following in the footsteps of the people he considered role models in the office was never going to bring him that fulfilment. After all, 33 years in, he was still waiting.

He took immediate action. Having chosen to take only about half his annual holiday allowance for as many years as he could remember, he announced that he was talking a four-week break. He and his wife spent a wonderful three weeks in the lakes and mountains of Italy, and the rest of the time was spent taking stock of his life.

He came back to me excited about the possibilities. He decided he was not ready to retire yet, but that he would start to prepare to do so within two to three years – much earlier than he had been planning. He was able to get transferred out of his demanding board-level job into a responsible yet much less stressful job in human resources. When I last saw him he had started evening classes in Italian, looking forward to another holiday and was excited about transitioning to flexible self-employment within a couple of years.

Unlike many unluckier people, Alan got his wake-up call in time. But why wait until you get that wake-up call? Much better to get your life into balance before you are presented with a make-or-break ultimatum. If you take an intelligent, happy frog and drop him into a pot of boiling water, what will the frog do? Jump out instantly! If you take the same frog and drop him into a pot of cold water, put the pot back on the stove and gradually heat up the pot, what then? He'll be merrily relaxing, thinking it's nice and warm here. Soon, you'll have a cooked frog. The moral of the story? Life happens gradually. Don't be fooled – be aware of what is really going on in your life.

SPIRITUALITY AT WORK

Spirituality, as I define it is simply a way of expressing more humanity. For me, spirituality means being true to myself, living lightly upon the earth and being inspired by a higher purpose. It is a sacred realm that is a natural, but often overlooked dimension of living itself. It is a way of experiencing the world that one can enter through special entry points. These entry points can be in nature such as mountaintops but also through a conscious awareness of a higher power. Spirituality has different meanings to different people. It has a lot to do with love, depth and reflection.

That which is spiritual:

- Creates alignment of purpose and people
- Comes from an inner knowing from the heart
- Creates an inner peace or 'centeredness'
- Is a *natural* desire to help others grow, learn, and succeed

What is spirituality at work? It is bringing the integrity, consideration, compassion and honesty we demonstrate when we are at our best into the office with us every day. It is mentoring others; even the smallest gesture can make a difference in helping another person believe in themselves. It is smiling at our colleagues and taking the time to get to know who they are *outside* of the organisation. It is the creativity, flow and passion we feel when engaged in an activity we love every time we sit down to work, because our work *is* something we love. For those in positions of power it is taking care not to abuse that power. It is treating employees in a responsible, caring way, and making the organisations we run socially responsible in terms of how they impact the environment, serve the community or create social change. From a material perspective, what we give away we lose. But from a spiritual perspective, only what we give away generously do we get to keep.

REFLECT

Ask yourself what work means to you:

- Something that you begrudge because it takes too much of your time?
- A necessary evil that pays the mortgage and expenses?
- A challenge that excites you?
- A means of self-expression?

If you answered yes to the first two and no to the last two, your way of thinking about work needs to be transformed. Once you are answering yes to the last two, the blocks to fulfilment at work will melt away.

The Corporate Condition

Let it 'Flow'

*"I never did a day's work in my
entire life. It was all fun."*

THOMAS EDISON, INVENTOR AND BUSINESSMAN

It's your first day back at work after your summer holiday.
You stare in disbelief at the pile of paperwork overflowing
on your in-tray. You sit down and switch on your computer
and are greeted with hundreds of e-mail messages awaiting
your attention. You bury your face in your hands and for a
moment are lost in memories – still fresh – of being by the
ocean with the wind blowing in your hair.

Reluctantly you open your eyes and a post-it note stuck to
your phone catches your attention: you need to call the
firm's most difficult, demanding client – the one no-one
wants to deal with. You listen to your voicemail: he has
been trying to contact you and has left a series of
increasingly impertinent messages. There is also a message
from your manager insisting you 'touch base' with him by
close of business. You let out a quiet sigh as thoughts of
leaving early today vanish.

As your blood pressure rises and the migraine starts to kick
in you momentarily reflect on the inner tranquillity that
pervaded your entire being during your relaxing family
break. Remembering the playful laughter in the pool leaves
you yearning to escape once again from the world of deals
and results. What happened to the 'dedicated and
enthusiastic' accolade in your appraisal? More to the point,

what happened to that lovely state of inner peace and harmony you experienced on holiday?

Have you ever wondered why it is that you become so… so… *human* when you are beside the sea walking hand in hand with your partner? You smile at travellers you meet on your journey and greet others as if they were souls you've known in another lifetime. Is this what the spiritual gurus refer to as the profound recognition of the spark of light in others? You interact fluidly with man and nature, appreciating and languishing in its beauty, so certain that there must be a master creator. You feel in awesome gratitude for the abundance of life. All is well within you. Appreciation comes easily. You are in the flow.

The good news is that it is possible to bring this state of 'flow' to work with you, every day. A silent inner knowing that this is something you would like to work towards is the first step.

TAPPING INTO THE FLOW AT WORK

The flow is a state of deep peace and connectivity. It is total immersion in an activity so that hours seem like minutes. It is working hard and enjoying it for the sheer joy of the work. Most importantly perhaps, it is being one hundred per cent in the present, with none of your mental energy focused on the past or the future. All of the above are common experiences of peak performers. When athletes talk about being 'in the zone' – and leaders in any sporting endeavour devote a lot of energy to being able to access this state at will – this is just another way of saying 'the flow'. Highly creative people tend to experience flow more often.

Think of the last time you experienced flow. Maybe you were relaxing on a beach, catching up with an old friend or engrossed in a great book. More interestingly, when was the last time you experienced 'flow' at work? How many times a day do you experience 'flow' while doing your job?

The first step is to pay close attention to what you are doing every day and notice how you feel emotionally doing different activities at work. I'm sure we are all likely to be happier at lunchtime! Some insights may come as a surprise, for example you may actually like the predictability of administration or working on your own. Some people may find they enjoy the interruption of calls to break their day up. We experience flow in our own unique way. Beethoven never heard his ninth symphony – he was stone deaf when he wrote it. Imagine what it must have felt like to have such a fire burning in the soul.

No doubt our surroundings affect our state of mind and we cannot all work by a lake or a mountain. We can however bring a little bit of nature into our offices. Maybe have a fish tank, pretty plants or crystals placed on tables and computers. Even getting rid of clutter can create a feeling of freedom and space.

It's an illusion to believe that we can leave parts of ourselves out of any environment or activity. Everything is personal. Why not be fully present? The personal evokes passion, creativity, and productivity. Every environment and every exchange offers an opportunity to deepen our spiritual work by putting it into practice.

Science has demonstrated that we don't end where our skin does. A field of energy extends beyond our body and affects everything around us. This energy can be negative and limited or positive and expansive. It is called *Chi* in Chinese and it is very powerful. Like attracts like, so when we are at ease and present in our work we radiate an expansive energy and we are treated in a far more positive way by others.

Creative artists have a wonderful way of letting go of judgments and open themselves up to use the 'wrong' colour. Ray Charles, one of the most talented musicians of our time, often frustrated his music company by creating music in a new style instead of one they could mass package and sell. As a result he was able to bring forth truly original works of art as he was in the 'flow'. If you surrender to the moment, remaining open to the creativity of the universe working through you, being spontaneous you will feel in the flow.

Often we don't know what our heart wants. To discover this and your next step stop thinking about it. Pursue something else. Spend free time doing something you truly love to do that you would not ordinarily do because you can't afford the time or the money to do it. It doesn't matter whether it's skiing, boating, painting, dreaming, hiking, running, or anything else. For each of us it's different, but it does matter that you know what it is that does it for you.

I remember as a teenager, when I started having regular sitar lessons at home and struggling in my first six months to play a few chords on an unusual and relatively complicated instrument. After this initial learning curve I began to understand the rhythms and nuances of Indian music and I started to give my fullest attention to playing with intensity. I felt a tremendous demand on my psychic energy but I was also totally focused, without the distracting thoughts of the initial months like, 'God, I'm never going to get this right,' or 'Damn, my finger is bleeding again and she still wants me to play another two ragas!' I was no longer self-conscious and I felt a remarkable sense of oneness with the instrument and the music. Hours seemed to pass by and I was lost in another zone that made me feel quite powerful. It wasn't necessarily easy either – I did feel emotionally and physically stretched. A remarkable side benefit was how much more confident I became in all other aspects of my life.

Does this mean that every time we are in the flow we are happy? Mihaly Csikszentmihalyi (pronounced 'Chick-sent-me high') in his highly researched book, *Finding Flow*, explains: *"It is the full involvement of flow, rather than happiness, that makes for excellence in life. When we are in flow, we are not happy, because to experience happiness we must focus on our inner states, and that would take attention away from the task at hand. If a rock climber takes time out to feel happy while negotiating a difficult move, he might fall to the bottom of the mountain... Only after the task is completed do we have the leisure to look back on what has happened, and then we are flooded with gratitude for the excellence of that experience – then, in retrospect we are happy. But one can be happy without experiencing flow. We can be happy experiencing the passive pleasure of a rested body, a warm sunshine, the contentment of a serene relationship. These are also moments to treasure, but this kind of happiness is very vulnerable and dependent on favourable external circumstances. The happiness that follows flow is of our own making, and it leads to increasing complexity and growth in consciousness."*

The truth is we spend little time truly loving what we do or doing what we love. Instead, we spend most of our time wishing that what we *are* doing could be more fulfilling. The reason for this is that we spend a lot of our time thinking about what we *would* be doing if we were happy rather than experiencing what it means to be joyful in the moment.

The most productive business planning is not only thinking about end results, but experiencing the journey. It's not about getting things, it's about becoming more human. It's not about winning or losing, it's about taking the time to stop during your climb up the mountain to breathe deeply and savour the intensely sweet joy of the moment. Don't wait till you're in the mood – do it anyway. It doesn't matter whether you are in the mood to be a world-class leader or be gracious to the office trainee today; do it anyway – and watch how it begins to lift your spirit.

In his book, *The Power Of Now*, Eckhart Tolle beautifully describes how living in the moment, you will be so much more alive to all experiences, to all sights and sounds. When you are fully here, it is so bold. We become bored with life because we think we know it all – yet we don't know anything! The reason we don't know anything is because every moment is new – and how could you know something that is always new? Life becomes exciting if you make each moment something new to experience. Play with your keyboard, stroke your cashmere jumper, tap your fingers to a tune on your desk, notice the ink that flows from your pen onto the paper and enjoy the buzz in your office! This newness is where your life source comes from. Life is never old or finished; it is as new and as young as the moment you were born. Loosen your attitudinal grip on the mundane and it will put you into a truer, more meaningful relationship with yourself no matter what type of work you are doing.

Spirituality is listening to our inner guidance and could be our greatest resource when making decisions.

Mindfulness simply means paying attention to what's happening right now. It can be difficult to do this in a busy office when we are over-stimulated. Building awareness of your emotional reality is extremely healthy, increases vitality and reduces stress. To build awareness learn to focus on your bodily sensations. For example, "I feel a knot in my stomach," could be a first step to acknowledging fear. Paying attention like this not only increases your awareness of your body and well-being, but can prevent unnecessary friction in the office. Once you can relax about your anxieties you can vocalise them in a calm manner which is assertive, not destructive.

I teach lunchtime meditation in the city and through reflective practice you can open up a new consciousness and a deeper purpose in life. You find that your natural instinct is refined and you can see the truth amidst the chaos and then make a judgment with breathtaking clarity. Meditation rests the mind the way sleep rests the body. My friend Carlos a regular meditator, works on the high-pressure trading floor. He firmly believes that he is not easily manipulated or fearful of fluctuating stocks because of this practice. It also makes it hard for power hungry bullies to intimidate a mindful person. I continue to be amazed at the wonderful changes in people who learned to really relax and go inside.

If you find yourself resisting any form of practice that slows you down and causes you to become more aware, it may be because your mind is struggling to repress a subconscious memory that it knows will cause you pain once you experience it. Allow yourself some space so that you can address it.

Remember the wisdom of Epicurus who teaches us about the three things human beings need to be happy. First is a sense of belonging in a community of friends. Second, freedom – the feeling that your life and choices are in your own hands. And third, a reflective life, which means having the time to ponder where you are going and what is important in life. We all need regular time in silence to connect with our inner voice.

REFLECT

HAIKU OF LIFE
A Haiku is a form of poetry that generally consists of three lines in which the first and last contain five syllables, while the middle is made up of seven. The subject is usually the natural world, a topic that tends to awaken us to our sense of onenesss with the divine. Here is an example written by the poet Chine:

It lights up
As lightly as it fades
A firefly

Try your hand at writing some haikus – but actually go out in nature and observe all the beauty around to inspire you.

TAKE OFF YOUR ARMOUR
We all now know the story really well: living amongst aggressions and anxieties of our society, we have to protect ourselves, put the armour on each morning after the cereal. At the end of the day when we are home safe and sound in our cocoon of security, the armour can come off – theoretically!

Unfortunately sometimes it gets stuck and won't come off and we end up alone without relief and rest. Try the following for peeling off that tight-fitting armour.

At night before you sleep, take off your clothes and while taking them off, imagine that you are not only taking off your clothes, but your armour too – with all the strains of the day falling off. Actually do it. Take it off and have a good deep breath – then go to sleep as if un-armoured, with nothing on the body and no restriction.

When you wake up the next day, instead of putting on the armour when you put your suit on, this time imagine your suit is made of helium light – in whatever colour you feel like wearing that morning. This is your protective light which is a gentle and friendly deterrent to predators. Imagine this light stays with you like a protective aura all day and notice how people react to you.

TEA BREAKS

Buddhists invented tea to help them with their meditation. Tea is therefore a sacred substance for Buddhists – as well as for the English! Zen has transformed the most ordinary activity into meditation. Even if you do not have a Zen tearoom in your office, you will be able to experience that deep reverence. Make it a ceremony; making tea or coffee... listening to the sound of the kettle, and then pouring the hot water, smelling the aroma of it, then tasting the drink and feeling peaceful and content. This moment you are alive! Feel thankful inside.

BE OPEN HANDED

This is another unusual action that we would never usually think to perform. It is very simple but enormously rewarding, especially if you are a hard-working business person.

Try placing your hands into the posture of a cup, like a receptacle. It is very meaningful, it helps you become receptive. It is one of the ancient Buddhist postures. Whenever you want to be open this will help. Sit silently and wait. Be a receptacle for abundance and joy, a receiving end. Just as you wait on the phone whilst you wait for your call to be answered. Just wait and within minutes you will notice a totally different energy surrounding you, filling your inside. There is a kind of softness and inner warmth and relief that results from such an unlikely act. Try doing it often in your hectic day and you will be surprised how much energy you will receive – it's all out there waiting for you after all.

MEETING OF THE HEARTS

We are so engrossed in our thoughts, worries and anxieties that very rarely do we meet someone with unassuming, non-judgmental eyes and with an open heart. This meeting is just a reflection of our tense minds and we are unable to connect with the other person. This simple method can help you immensely in all your relationships.

When you have a business meeting, settle within yourself, become silent. When your client or business contact arrives, feel a deep peace for them and welcome them with a smile. When you shake their hands look into their eyes and connect on a deeper level. You will find a much more satisfactory connection based on honesty, trust and friendliness. Remember the Hindu tradition of greeting with a 'namaste' – it means 'I honour the soul in you'.

WORK WISE

A great part of our lives are spent at the office working, yet how many of us really enjoy working? We work as a duty and wait for the weekends and holidays to finally relax and take our masks off. Yet if we could bring a contented relaxation to our work, we will discover that work is actually not work, but is both pleasure and meditation!

This is a simple method that will bring a new quality of enjoyment into your work. Do this everyday if you can and soon you will see there is no difference between a business deal and playing with your children!

Whenever you feel in a bad mood and you feel a bit stressed out, before you start your day, just for five minutes breathe deeply. With every in breath, imagine breathing in positive light energy. With every strong exhalation, feel that you are releasing your dark mood out which is like a grey cloud floating away. It is simply a shift of emphasis, very simple and easy to do. You will start to do things more carefully and lovingly.

EXPERIENCE YOUR OWN SPACE

Working in a large office can mean we are always surrounded by an intense people-filled environment. Tale a moment out of your day to experience an oasis of peace, by walking near some trees and feeling the earth beneath your feet. This will ground you. Some people also feel a calmness while washing their hands and allowing the flowing water to cleanse away any overwhelming emotions. Creating this space for yourself will help you energise for the challenges ahead.

Let It Flow

34

Materialism & Maya:
Weapons of Mass Delusion

"It is preoccupation with possessions, more than anything else, that prevents us from living freely and nobly."

HENRY DAVID THOREAU, AMERICAN POET AND PHILOSOPHER

Why do you work? Think about it for a few minutes. At least part of your reason is very likely to be financial. Have you ever felt like the proverbial rat on the treadmill funding mortgages, private education and the trappings of so-called success? Many people are finding themselves in the middle of a collective debt ridden nightmare that's uninspired and unsustainable… one that's making them feel as if they are slowly being sucked into a dark whirlpool. In the corner of their consciousness, a faint voice whispers, 'there must be more to life than this'.

The Sanskrit word 'maya' means illusion, a veiling of the true reality. Consider an illusion in the dark of a rope being confused as a venomous snake. While we've been told that creating material success will make us feel good, some of my multi-millionaire clients admit that they were shocked by how empty their triumphs are and how their riches didn't fill an inner gap. This is accompanied by the fear of losing what they have accumulated and so they frantically try to protect it. Protection comes in many forms; insurance cover is one thing but there is also the temptation to compromise ourselves and go for the hard sell. An estate agent friend confided in me that he feels physically sick in having to lie to his clients when his commission is at stake and now realises he needs to change career for the sake of his sanity.

We interact in an outside world where everything is pervaded by considerations of monetary worth. Consider the hypnotic power that is exerted over us by a sleek red Ferrari or a huge mansion with a tennis court and swimming pool, overlooking the ocean.

What happens to us and inside us when we imagine or see these images in the media? The intensity of our emotions is raised by bonuses, designer labels and items of luxury. This buying into a lifestyle concept is exploited magnificently by marketing gurus to create glamour and illusion. It is like a drug and we become addicted over time. Are we buying into it? Look around you – what do you think?

What do we imagine these increased riches will really do for us? What is realistic and what is illusory in the power we attribute to wealth? Will it give us more power, more friends, make us become God? We think that financial success will protect us from harm; from being without food and shelter and from having to depend on others. Sadly, these dreams are unsustainable – even if we built up a massive nest egg, it wouldn't protect us from becoming terminally ill or losing our child in an accident.

A few years ago I was introduced to a portly merchant banker at a networking event who, in between panama cigars, had to swallow tablets for his nerves. Throughout the evening he just couldn't stop name dropping and bragging about his growing portfolio; his influence over 'keen to please' politicians, open to discrete bribery which had enabled him to extend his business empire across the city. I politely listened, bemused by his own trumpet blowing and intrigued by such open self-declaration. It's as if he needed a witness to his story. What followed in our conversation saddened me a little, as I learned about his true loss. When I asked him about his family his face flushed with the raw tinge of shame as his eyes darted to his Rolex. He only just realised that he had failed to make it to his disabled daughter's first swimming competition that evening. I suspect this happened all too often in his world. Here is a classic example of a man who has been too busy making money to spend time with his loved ones.

When we fear we don't have enough – enough time, money, friends and so on - we are participating in the nightmare of scarcity. Such anxieties can lead to a deeper turbulence. A surprising number of my clients recall memories of being disturbed for days after having a nightmare in which they were a haggard old bag lady roaming the streets at night, completely destitute and hungry. Psychologists tell us that this is a very common dream. Such fears of scarcity creep in at times. Yet we have so much and not enough. Conflicts begin to fester inside of us.

Many of us go shopping every day, not because we have to but because we want to believe that if we buy something we'll have 'enough'. In order to awaken from this illusion we need to reject the poorly written script that dictates, "Once I have_____, I will be happy". While you are striving to achieve more try to hold onto the vision that you are enough and are surrounded by plenty. This will help you manifest your dream from a solid place.

There is something about the human psyche that feels the need for approval. To redecorate our colossal house we will re-mortgage and stretch ourselves so that it's good enough to impress our relatives and neighbours. Until we decide that other people's opinions will no longer dictate how we live our life; until we prefer the luxury of being the master of our own world; and until we conclude that life's too short to be enslaved by anything or anybody, least of all by smooth talking marketers, we will be susceptible to the largest epidemic since biblical times: *status anxiety*. In his satirical and humorous novel of the same title, author Alain de Botton wrote: *"The anxiety is provoked by, among other elements, recession, redundancy, promotions, retirement, conversations with others in the same industry, newspaper profiles of the prominent, and the greater success of friends. [...] Evidence of the inner drama is uncommon, limited usually to a preoccupied gaze, a brittle smile, or an over-extended pause after news of another's achievement."*

Confusion sets in and we create pleasurably intense fantasies in our minds of extreme luxury. How many of us if we are honest can admit to moments of weakness when we have envied the wild, hedonistic lifestyle of the rich and famous? How wonderful would it be to have the freedom to do anything we wanted at any time? But how did that thought get inside of us? We probably don't remember letting it in. It may seem natural to drift away like this but do we really need so much and if so *why?* Looking at it rationally and truthfully, just how much of our time is swallowed up by unrealistic fantasies like winning the lottery? Wonderful as it may make us feel at the time there is a need to balance this with a focus on all that we *do* have. Bless the money you have and be open to receiving money from unexpected avenues.

CHECK INSIDE: ARE YOU
COMPENSATING FOR SOMETHING?

If you think you could not live without your impressive job title or sports car keep this in mind: it is not the job title or the car that your soul yearns for, but the *feelings* these things give you. That can be a range of things, from security and comfort to excitement and challenge. There is, in my opinion, one thing underlying it all: a gnawing self-esteem issue at the root of the problem. People simply don't feel they are *enough* – good enough, smart enough, successful enough, attractive enough – and that's why they need external 'props'.

So much of our energy goes into 'looking good' in front of others and we tend to pursue whatever it is we think will secure us the approval and status we hunger for. The plastic surgery is often just elastoplast over a deep and, it seems, universal psychological wound. It speaks of a deep insecurity, a feeling that you are not adequate and need validation to be on this earth. We may find it helpful instead to make a conscious decision to find less costly, not to mention more direct, routes to fulfilment.

Ask yourself, "What do I feel I need to have to signal how very important I am?"

Financial hardship causes people more emotional problems than almost any other life issue. How many times have you heard that 'Money doesn't grow on trees', that 'Money is the root of all evil' or that anyone who is rich must, by definition, be either a crook or arrogant? Many people have negative associations about wealth and money that were gained subconsciously whilst growing up.

Let's not make the puritanical mistake of equating money with evil and poverty with good. It's great to be rich. Be ambitious - be rich inside and out. If the world is ever made better, it will be made so by people of conscience with money. Money in itself is neither good nor bad – we attribute the element of impurity to it. It is the mind that is the source of greed and money is one of the places where it expresses itself. It is our attachment to money that is the issue.

Money is a symbolic medium of exchange among humanity, to represent accumulated creative energy. It symbolises energy flow. To see it as a sacred trust to be used for the good of all humanity is the highest view of it.

You can't take your money with you when you die! We have all heard that saying. From a higher perspective, we can ultimately possess nothing on the material level – although it might possess us because we are too attached to it or worried about it! Nothing truly belongs to us – it's all on loan from the universe during this lifetime. When you understand that we take nothing material with us you can begin to see how travelling lightly on this earth is so liberating.

We can be good custodians of what we have been blessed with. We can keep our resource channels clear and flowing and harmonised with the universal laws. When we care for and improve what has been entrusted to us, and release to others things that we no longer use, we see a new inflow of abundance. If only the banks had treated public money with this level of custodianship, instead of allowing individuals to grow fabulously rich making failed bets with other people's money.

We have seen examples in the media of how the self-absorbed life focused on personal indulgence leads to disillusionment and finally, despair. I wonder what obsessive thoughts the disgraced US financier Bernard Madoff had as he continued to steal from his investors.

Those who create a set of higher values around having money – values such as generosity, taking responsibility and integrity - discover they are living life at its deepest level. Interestingly, before the G20 Summit in 2009, Gordon Brown, the UK prime minister made an extraordinary appeal for everyday family values to be applied to the financial system. He said, *"In our families we raise our children to work hard and to do their best and do their bit. We don't reward them for taking risks that would put them or others in danger and we don't encourage them to seek short-term gratification at the expense of long-term value."*

TAKING RESPONSIBILITY CAN PUT YOU ON THE MAP

Robert Kiyosaki is a man who added to the wealth he had created through property and other business deals by writing about his two dads – one rich, one poor. *(Rich Dad, Poor Dad: What The Rich Teach Their Kids About Money That The Poor And Middle Class Do Not!)* Back in the early 1970s he was getting rich on the back of other people's misery and poverty. His lifestyle made him a magnet for beautiful women, fast cars and invitations to the hippest parties. Yet he found out that although his rich dad had taught him how to make money, he had failed to find deep personal meaning and fulfilment through living purposefully.

"When Buckminster Fuller asked me what my purpose in life was, I honestly didn't know. What I did realise was that I couldn't continue getting rich from Korean factories

populated with child labour", says Kiyosaki. *"I hate poverty, and what ultimately caused me to quit rock and roll merchandising was when I saw those young kids squatting with their knees up to their ears in order to increase the square footage so I could make more products and get more money."* He now educates children about finances and it costs him around $2 million a year to make his *'Cashflow For Kids'* game available to any recognised educational institution in the world.

The big question on all our lips is how to achieve financial security with some spiritual component. More of us are questioning what we were put on this earth to do. Is it really to play golf all day or to watch reality TV most evenings? *"Money does not make you, it reveals you,"* Kiyosaki concludes. *"We're not here to make money, we're here to solve the world's problems and make life better for everyone. That purpose goes on, even when you have money. Likewise, a key ingredient for making money is being of service to humanity. That's the ninety degree approach that will fill the hole in your soul."*

On a deeper level some people evolve much better in poverty. They will move when in extremity, but do nothing when things are pleasant. You will always be presented with what is needed for your growth. If poverty brings up fears for you – that's okay. You can use this for your spiritual development. There is nothing wrong with being poor, except in feeling poor.

PUTTING PASSION FIRST

A client of mine – I'll call her Milly – was a senior executive at a leading PR firm, but her passion lay elsewhere. Now in her forties, she had loved animals since she was a child and was an active supporter and campaigner for several animal welfare organisations. A year or so earlier she had begun devoting her PR services for free to one charity, and found that this work inspired and motivated her like nothing she had ever done before. In the meantime her day job had become much less fulfilling with long hours, too much travel and a work environment she disliked intensely.

Worse still, her firm did PR for several companies which exploited animals, such as a fashion house which used real fur and a pharmaceutical company which used animals for experiments. When she was told to manage an account for the former, she realised that she could no longer stay at this company as the work she was being asked to do was so at odds with her ethics and values. I sensed in Milly a compassionate philanthropist who wanted to make a difference in the world.

Milly was a real goal setter, understanding that without them, the future chooses us. We started by looking at her Wheel of Life. This helped her identify goals in eight key areas: physical environment, health, money, personal growth, recreation, relationships, work and family. Under each of the headings she rated her level of satisfaction on a scale of 0 (totally unsatisfied) to 10 (totally satisfied). There were some interesting surprises for her! We looked at what she needed to do and was willing to do to increase the lower ratings.

Next, we researched what her options were. Although she was open to other paths, she was so excited about the possibility of a career in the animal welfare field that we concentrated on this first. She already knew that she would be taking a huge salary cut, but I got her to research specifically what she could expect to earn in this sector and whether that was realistic for her. The result: she would be earning less than a quarter of what she earned today, with only modest and gradual salary increases and no expectation of ever reaching her current level nor even close to it.

However, as Milly was single with no children, her mortgage was paid off and she had a healthy portfolio of savings and investments, she was willing to take the cut. In fact, by this time, she told me, she was so passionate that she would work in this field for free! Being paid any amount, however small, seemed like a bonus to her. She would have to cut her spending a great deal, but that didn't matter, she told me, as much of her spending was tied up with the lifestyle her job imposed on her: designer clothes, salon treatments, socialising with colleagues at the best clubs and restaurants in town, and so on.

The next step was for Milly to look at the charities she could approach and research the positions available. She decided that although she'd enjoyed her time with the organisation she'd been doing volunteer PR work for, it wasn't the one for her as it was in a busy part of London and she wanted to move out of the city. She homed in on a charity in Sussex that was looking for a press officer. A month later she was offered the job, and she hasn't looked back since. She has exchanged her flat in London for a house by the sea and on our last coaching call she told me that she feels much richer than she has ever felt in her life. The change I saw Milly experience in a short time was dramatic, yet the first seeds of it had been sown many, many years earlier.

Why do some people give up lucrative jobs for a riskier endeavour? They do it because the latter fires their souls and opens the way for unrealised potential. As they say, purpose and passion – discover one and you find the other and often they have nothing to do with the money.

A report prepared by investment bank Dresdner Kleinwort Wasserstein in November 2005 provides a mass of evidence that shows that people who focus on more materialistic goals are less happy and healthy than those who prioritise relationships or personal growth. Spending on experiences rather than items makes people happier. Therefore, money is best channelled into activities with friends and family like concerts and holidays, rather than being used to amass possessions like a fast car, bigger house or a designer bag. The report also found that: *"Not only are people who pursue materialistic goals setting themselves up for a generally unfulfilling experience, but they are considerably more prone to mental anguish and problems as well."*

In the words of Lao Tzu:

Chase after money and security

And your heart will never unclench

Care about people's approval

And you will be their prisoner

Do your work, then step back

The only path to serenity

BRINGING MORE OF OURSELVES INTO THE GAME

People often ask me how it is possible to make the sales process of transferring a product or service to another in exchange for money into a meaningful transaction involving the heart. I remind them that the important thing to remember is that with every project or sale, you are making a connection with someone else. Without that connection there would be no sale. The essence of spirituality is being in the present. The essence of a successful connection is your ability to be in the present.

This means being able to tune into the other person's needs, feelings and thoughts. From a spiritual perspective every connection with another person is an opportunity to be of service. When we provide a service that truly benefits others, without creating harm anywhere, then a fair and equitable profit for the work done is in order. Profit allows this service or product to continue to be provided to others.

The famous spiritual text *A Course In Miracles* puts it beautifully: *"When you meet anyone, remember it is a holy encounter. As you see him, you will see yourself. As you treat him, you will treat yourself. Never forget this, for in him, you will find or lose yourself."*

Many people have a life goal that is bigger than themselves - they have a cause beyond personal wealth and pleasure. A cause that will touch the lives of others and bring meaning to their work. US chat show host Oprah Winfrey once wrote in *Oprah* magazine: *"Use me, God. Show me how to take who I am, who I want to be, and what I can do, and use it for a purpose greater than myself."* Many successful leaders in business, such as Jeffrey Swartz of Timberland Shoes, have demonstrated the power of living their values. Swartz pays his employees to volunteer in the community.

Mother Teresa said that there are no great acts, only small acts performed with great love. Yet too often we aspire *to be* the next Mother Teresa without the sacrifice or dedication. Instead of wanting to make a difference in the world and seeing opportunities for doing so, we have a grandiose goal and proclaim, "I want to make a billion pounds so I can rescue the starving children". After all, a billion pounds symbolises great power doesn't it? Again, we get fixated on symbols of success.

REFLECT

What is of ultimate value? What is there that is not a means to something? What do you pursue for its own sake alone? For me, its things like creativity, love, beauty and connection with others. These are the treasures just waiting to be grabbed that give life so much meaning and satisfaction. When the shallowness of materialism becomes self-evident, these things remain and continue to deliver their promise.

Ask yourself the following questions:

- Will the world be better for my having been here?
- Do I need to leave my deepest values at the workplace door?
- What will last when my work is over?
- What could I start doing straight away to bring more meaning to my life? Teach English to orphans in Africa? Campaign for reduced toxic emissions?

- If I continue to live my life this way, will I be able to look back – in one year, five years, twenty years – and feel a sense of honour and integrity about what I have created?

- When I get up in the morning and come face-to-face with myself, do I like who I've become? Am I a living model of the very things I say are important in my life?

- Am I the example I would want my children to follow?

The Corporate Mask

"The challenge for business leaders in the twenty-first century is to assume the mantle of spiritual elder for their cultures, so that life doesn't become trivial and grey for all the people who spend most of their life at work."

JIM CHANNON, AUTHOR AND THE BUSINESS WORLD'S FIRST CORPORATE SHAMAN

There was a time when companies, even big ones, were like families and employees were cared for like children. Loyalty and competence were enough to get you through and you could even expect a job for life. The employer-employee relationship was one based on loyalty and mutual respect. But those days are now long gone, booted into touch by years of restructuring and heavy redundancies.

With the IT revolution, many of us are excited by the rapid developments, but at the same time feel uncertain and vulnerable. This is where seeking strength in spirituality and human connection can play a very beneficial part.

The greatest spiritual challenge arises when we are part of an organisation which has a dysfunctional culture. Employees at all levels have the responsibility to influence this reality and make it healthy. Spirituality at work requires that we work to change the culture so that sound business practices are followed. When confronted with the challenge of shaping corporate culture, it is important to follow the advice of Reinhold Niebuhr, seeking the *"serenity to accept the things we cannot change, the courage to change those that we can, and the wisdom to know the difference."*

How do you get clear about the cultural values in your organisation? Attitudes reveal values – so begin by noticing the prevailing attitudes around you in the office. Often the cultural values of our workplace influence us in subtle ways. Becoming more aware of these influences can free us to choose when we will support these values and when we will offer an alternative.

PRECIOUS TIME

In *The Age of Paradox*, Charles Handy states that modern industry has turned time into a commodity. Our culture is almost obsessed with time: finding enough of it, making the most of it, saving more of it. But even with all the attention we give it, we're rarely truly mindful of how we spend it.

- Are you expected to put in long hours and pay your dues to earn your partnership or directorship? If you don't, are you considered unprofessional, uncooperative and unwilling to renounce your self-interest for the greater good of the organisation? Do you risk losing promotion, pay rises or even perhaps your very job?

- Do you have to stay at your desk after normal working hours? Are client needs paramount in terms of unrestricted availability and tight deadlines?

- Do you sometimes stay at work even though you have nothing to do just because you want to be seen to be 'putting in the hours'? In some companies there in an unspoken rule that says if you leave before a certain time you are not a dedicated employee.

A client of mine who is a financial journalist once confided in me about the above. When she started her traineeship as an enthusiastic graduate she planned to get her work done between 9:00 and 5:30, the hours on her contract. Evenings, as far as she was concerned, were for socialising, going to the gym or the movies or just relaxing and unwinding at home. But she soon realised this wasn't to be and it was nothing to do with the workload.

On her first day, she threw herself into the work and was way ahead of schedule for meeting all of the first week's deadlines when she turned off her computer at the end of the day. She had noticed that her new colleagues did not seem that motivated and that their desks were not exactly hives of activity. She was the only person to skip out of the office at 5:30 pm; no one else made the slightest move. The following day was the same. On the Wednesday of her first week she cancelled the plans she had made for that night and stayed put, curious to see what time the others would leave.

At seven o'clock everyone was still there. She had no work that needed doing, so spent her time surreptitiously observing her colleagues. One was leafing through a tabloid newspaper. Others were engaged in emailing or talking to friends. She noticed that others were also nervously looking around checking what everyone else was doing.

When she had been there a couple of weeks the features editor who sat behind her confided that it was not the 'done thing' to leave before 7.00 pm, and if you were really serious you'd stay much later. Anyone who wanted to please the managers had better put in the hours, regardless of whether they had anything to put *into* those hours. Soon, she found herself working less effectively during the day because there was no incentive to get work done quickly.

More and more firms now give employees realistic workloads and encourage them to get out in the world and develop other parts of themselves once their work is done. Such firms breed a much more efficient, stable, well-rounded workforce. Which is the more effective employee? Someone who is efficient and motivated during the working day, and leads a happy and fulfilling life? Or is it the stressed, miserable employee who lacks both the efficiency and the well-roundedness of the 'clock-watchers'?

Whilst working in New York as a junior lawyer I was required to carry a pager around with me after working hours in case I was needed urgently to finalise contracts for this very important multi-national client. I was enjoying dinner on a Saturday night with friends and had to leave my delicious cappuccino cheesecake halfway, to rush back to the office, only to find that the matter could have easily waited until Monday morning!

Later on, back in London, I worked for a firm that had rooms with beds on the top floor, a gym and breakfast bar. The underlying message: "You don't need to go home! If you're not sleeping you should be here working. Why waste time commuting?" This may be an extreme example, but many firms have unspoken policies that encourage employees to become one-dimensional corporate robots with little time for loved ones or hobbies.

ETHICAL PLAYING FIELD

- Is acting with integrity encouraged or is it a *lack* of ethics that gets rewarded by your firm?

- Could you challenge the status quo where you feel that others are not acting with integrity?

- Do the values of your workplace or profession run counter to your own values or to the values of your spiritual tradition?

- Are their websites/marketing literature consistent?

Joe Tye, author of the book, *Staying On Top: When The World's Upside Down,* offers this advice for staying true to your ethics at work: *"In a way that does not impose your own religious beliefs upon others, commit yourself to being an example of someone who lives according to high moral values and deep spiritual faith."*

As a trainee working on the pensions fraud scandal in the early 1990s, I was stunned each time I saw my supervising partner routinely treble the amount our client owed and quote that number on the invoice. This, of course, would ultimately be at the expense of the poor pensioners who had already lost so much. When I gingerly challenged the partner, he went red in the face; not out of embarrassment, but out of anger. "It's a complex case," he snapped. "That is reflected in the £300 an hour fee," I wanted to reply. Yet I was all too aware how risky such boldness would be.

How many of us allow a huge gap to exist between the values of our private lives and the values of the workplace? Community, contribution, generosity, love and sincerity may be important to us at home, but in the workplace we are often rewarded for independence, competition and acquisition. This is ideal breeding ground for jealousy and toxic emotions.

If your spiritual values are important to your mental well-being, then at some point you will have to take a stand. In today's climate, even in a downturn you can afford to be a visible example of your own spiritual values. Tolerance for unethical behaviour is lowering. You must decide whether you can live with any gulf between your ethics and those of your organisation. In the end, integrity always pays off and if it does not happen at your current firm, you will soon outgrow that firm and move on to somewhere more in line with your ethics.

SPACE MATTERS

Your work environment and the space you have around you are vital to your well-being – this allows you breathing space and the freedom to get on with things. Companies like Intel Corp and Coca-Cola Co provide space for workplace Bible classes as well as for other religious groups. *Thinking space for senior staff is also important – a chance for reflection away from the hothouse.*

- Are you crammed in the office with potential health and safety hazards or do you have a comfortable work environment?

- Do you have plants, air-conditioning and water tanks for your comfort?

- Is there a cafeteria or kitchen, and if so is it a spacious, friendly, bright place people like to congregate during work breaks – or not?

- Are there any relaxation facilities such as quiet rooms, a meditation room, a gym?

INCLUSIVE COMMUNICATION

Communication is the tool that allows people to work together. In our society our learning process is based on communicating with teachers and parents (usually, by learning how to *avoid* punishment). When we go out into the world most of us have not learned how to communicate with our peers for the purpose of achieving something beneficial for all of us. We constantly try to win the favour of the 'parent' or 'teacher' or 'adult' – usually a management figure. We try not to get punished.

This behaviour leads to subterfuge among employees: trying to work out how to beat the system, gain extra favours, say the popular thing or to keep our views to ourselves rather than 'rock the boat'. Our true voice is lost. Just imagine instead what it would be like if we were rewarded for being more or even totally truthful in the workplace – honest self-expression would flourish.

Ask yourself:

- Can you discuss anything, including your feelings about work and non-work issues with management?

- Is there a forum for two-way discussion between employees and management?

- Do management have an open-door policy; i.e. are they easily approachable? Or are they shut away on another floor of the building, and unreceptive to staff approaching *them?*

As an executive coach I work with many high performers who for one reason or another go through some real lows at work. One thing that they often say is how little their organisation really cares about them. They complain that the relationship at work is purely an economic one and if only they were more nurtured, that would release so much more of their inner potential which is just waiting for expression. If we feel that our firm values and respects us, it counts for a lot when deciding whether or not we stay in our jobs. This is only possible if there is an open channel of communication between management and employees.

Where Truth Stands

"A single lie destroys a whole reputation for integrity."

BALTASAR GRACIAN, SPANISH PROSE WRITER
& AUTHOR OF THE ART OF WORDLY WISDOM

When truth is compromised, trust and confidence begin to break down. It becomes acceptable for staff to tell lies in order to step up the ladder of success. Substance starts to matter less than subterfuge; reality less than perception.

Common examples of lies include:

- "Tell the customer what he wants to hear. All that matters is the sale."

- "Your job is secure," (followed by the person being made redundant).

- "You *will* get positive results in this research project. We need the grant to be renewed."

- "That was not sexual harassment. It was just a bloke being a bloke. Ignore him."

- Do different people give consistent answers to the same question? Are they looking for honest answers or trying to second guess what you want to hear? Second guessing suggests that the habit of honesty has faded.

PROTECTIVE ARM OF FAIRNESS

We all want to compete on a level playing field, but do we all ascribe to equal opportunity regardless of race, sex, age, religion, or disability in the real world? The answer is obviously not often enough. Discrimination can happen via the informal systems of the old boy's network, or the unseen glass ceiling. Abuse in the form of discrimination is hidden but very real. It flies in the face of the myth that all of us are created with equal opportunity. Just imagine how loyal and productive people would be to a system that treated them fairly.

Ever come across any of these: discrimination, overwork, harassment, systematic humiliation, withholding of resources, financial manipulation, hidden agendas and smothering big brother policies? What do they have in common? They all have their human cost. What sort of human cost? Stress, headaches, nervous breakdowns, heart attacks – all have been linked to working environments that breed fear and hostility. There is also the effect on relationships, families and self-esteem.

Ask yourself:

- Do women have to work twice as hard as men to get the same promotional opportunities?

- Do management often exclude minorities such as non-whites and gays?

- Does your age matter when it comes to the issue of promotion?

CREATIVE FREEDOM

Creativity includes the use of imagination, laughter and freedom to enhance productivity. Creativity is fun and when people enjoy what they do, they work much harder. It includes conscious efforts to see things differently, to break out of habits and to let go of out-dated beliefs to find new ways of thinking, doing and being. People are naturally creative but when they are forced to crush their creativity, the repressed energy force turns to destructive release, as their inherent humanity needs to express itself.

Ask yourself:

- Do you get credit for your good ideas?
- Are you encouraged to suggest changes for improvement?
- Are you allowed to experiment and make mistakes, or does fear of getting things wrong stifle creativity?

GREAT CORPORATE COMMUNITIES

A lot of effort goes into making companies look inviting, successful and fun. Many companies now provide a wide array of work-life balance programs. They place great verbal emphasis on healthy employees. Gyms, health clubs and childcare provision all suggest that companies will keep your best interests at heart.

Yet the question I am most often asked is: How can I tell whether a particular company will be a great place to work? Somehow the buildings and the policies don't seem to answer that question. Most often, I'm asked the question by women who are constantly trying to read between the lines to find out whether a company is female friendly.

What you see is not always what you get. It seems to get harder and harder to get a true picture of a company before you join. Great places to work are not about skyscrapers, mahogany boardrooms and corporate jets; they are about great *communities*.

Here are some aspects that employees who are going for interviews should look out for – and that employers who want to hire loyal, competent and discerning staff need to pay attention to:

- Does the interviewee get a chance to meet people at different levels of the organisation and ask questions? A culture of openness and trust is evident when things are done openly, for instance, doors are generally open, there are open areas and glass panels where meetings can be seen.

- Is there a distinct hierarchy? For instance, do only the junior staff fetch the coffee? My boss often used to ask the team if he could get us a drink when he popped out for a bite to eat. We felt really good that he had no qualms about this at all.

- Are the diversity policies fair? As an interviewee, can you see people like yourself in the top levels of management? If you are female, black, disabled or gay and don't see anyone like that on the board or at least at higher managerial levels, you would be entitled to be pretty sceptical about diversity policies.

- Does the corporate social responsibility policy really do something?

- Employees are keen to find out the take up rate of sabbaticals and maternity/paternity/stress leave policies. Work-life balance is increasingly important to both the sexes. Is there an unspoken, hidden price attached to taking leave? Even younger employees who do not have children now are still concerned about what happens when they do. What happens when elderly parents need us?

- Do people openly talk about outside hobbies or holidays? Does the sparkle in their eyes remain when the conversation reverts to work?

- Who are the heroes and villains of the office? Those who are admired will show us *what* is admired.

ENGAGING YOUR PEOPLE

In looking at corporate cultures, perhaps the greatest single indicator of all is retention: How long do people stay with the company? In companies with fast staff turnover no one builds strong relationships – what's the point if your colleagues are going to leave next year?

It's very typical for corporate objectives which see the company as being full of bouncy enthused 'can do' staff with real proactive business attitude, who are determined, empowered and incentivised. How do you 'walk the talk'? Often Directors are dedicated to ensuring clients feel rewarded in bringing their business to the company. They are all busily engaged in helping clients. Being personally too busy with client work to make enough time to help and nurture the rest of your people is something to think about.

Many companies are finding the most effective way to bring spiritual values into the workplace is to clarify the company's vision and mission, and to align it with a higher purpose and deeper commitment to service to both customers and community. But be careful of those platitudes. You know – lofty ones that make you cringe!

More companies are being forced to offer workplace conditions that support life overall: not just on the job, but in the area of personal well-being and quality of life. Companies are moving away from blanket solutions that might not suit every worker – such as granting specific religious days off – to more subtle accommodations like quiet rooms and use of company computer networks for faith groups.

In today's environments, it is not just money that keeps people attached to their place of work. Recent research by Tim Osborn-Jones, Henley Management College's expert in organisational behaviour, proved that the economic part of a manager's benefits package does not carry as much weight as the non-financial elements. *"My evidence is that most managers are still looking for a relationship with their employers. They want a more effective relationship with issues such as aspiration, equity and community remaining important. My argument is that for those who have the talent and can make a choice this is what counts."* Employees are becoming much better informed about what ties them down and what doesn't.

Corporate and personal growth comes through responsible change. Your organisation may have it's problems, but instead of justifying continuing outdated, old patterns, blaming others for the way it is, you need to take charge. Assess your workplace, see that there is a need for change and start that process.

Every evening the main asset of your company walks out of the door. Let's make sure the best people come back the next morning, and keep coming back.

REFLECT

- What three words would you use to describe the principle values of your workplace or profession?

- Are the values actually practiced differently than the 'stated values' or mission statement of your organisation?

- How has your workplace or profession shaped you since you began your work?

- Have you noticed that things once very important to you are less so now?

- How have you shaped, or could you shape, your workplace culture?

- Does your workplace encourage, tolerate or discourage diverse and individual perspectives? How? What could be improved?

Where Truth Stands

Team Play

"Never doubt that a small group of thoughtful,
committed people can change the world. Indeed,
it is the only thing that ever has."

MARGARET MEADE, CULTURAL ANTHROPOLOGIST

It is an oft-quoted story that in the USA nine finalists with disabilities were competing for a gold medal when half way round the track one of them fell. He tried so hard to get up, only to fall again. He tried again without success. Finally he just lay there and began to sob. One by one the other contestants heard his sobbing and stopped running. They headed back and helped him up. All the contestants then held hands, walked down the track and crossed the finish line together. The crowd were thrilled – they couldn't believe their eyes. They rose and gave a 15-minute standing ovation.

When I first read this I was so moved. This was one of our finest moments; humanity at its best. We are all capable of such great heights. Deep down it feels right when we step in to help out a fellow human in need. This is not an intellectual sort of knowing. This is the way of the heart. When we feel deeply, we are dealing with the soul. It is as if our soul is in heaven at that moment. We can help fellow colleagues who might be struggling with a sales pitch or need some guidance on how to handle a complex project. It need not be so dramatic that you get a standing ovation for your efforts!

Have you noticed how the desperation for success sometimes brings out the baser primitive survival instinct?

They don't call it the urban jungle for nothing! Our hearts sink and our souls constrict when we continuously endure the ruthlessness of a cutthroat and competitive work culture.

We become less interested in achieving higher standards in our work and more keen to protect our positions through deceptive ploys and defensive tactical moves. At such times our vision is clouded by fear and suspicion. We cannot even come alive at home as this state of mind we have in our jobs has robbed us of so much energy that there is nothing left to give. Our spouse and children see us exhausted and at times we cannot cope and our tempers run short at the smallest request from them.

A self-preservation work culture has led us to construct protective, artificial shields in front of our hearts. Fear turns our creative, fertile minds into a wasteland and transforms normally reasonable people into bullies. You only need to read a few employment law cases to appreciate the unhappy outcomes.

Remember the scene in the movie Star Wars where Luke Skywalker confronts the dark side of The Force in a tunnel, and it turns out to be a reflection of himself? We all have a darker side which is most likely to emerge in a tough environment.

It is hardly surprising that so many people have issues in this area. In school, we learn 'team' work by competing with each other and competing with other teams. We aren't usually taught the kind of true teamwork that involves everyone emerging as a winner and an equal. No, it's about finishing first, coming out on top, defeating the opponent. Unless we are incredibly aware and conscientious, we carry this conditioning into our workplaces. In a culture that overvalues individuality, we're taught that we should stand out from the crowd. Caught up in this game we start to desire thunderous applause and validation of our tremendous importance at the office.

More and more great leaders of our day find that the best way to work is to draw on the strength of others, to build teams and to develop synergy. After all, it gets lonely achieving goals on your own. To bring a team together and see the dream realised together brings community to success and vice-versa. How about we forget about ladders to the top? Think instead of a group journey on a boat with everyone supporting each other. And if anyone accidentally falls overboard there will always be someone ready to jump in to save him. This is the 'You win, I win' attitude. Individual success should not mean the failure of others.

Roger Salient, CEO of Plug Power, one of the first electric fuel cell companies says that work at his organisation *"[...] is not your job or my job. It's our job. And that's how people become enlisted when we are working together. It's what happens when you think of yourself having no boundaries, when you think of yourself as working in a field of connection and consciousness."*

When a group of people are committed to a common purpose, are given responsibility, and at the same time feel supported and trusted, then, and only then, will they tap their deepest potential.

When we stay connected to the larger group and regularly experience ourselves as part of the whole, we can exchange wisdom and help each other much faster. When we are competitive – we are isolated. Quantum theory shows that there are forms of exchanging information that we can't perceive with our senses yet are very real, allowing us to connect with each other. For example, a particularly clever bird, the blue-tit made a huge discovery a few decades ago. By tapping its beak against the foil seal of the milk bottles sitting on the doorsteps it could drink the cream floating on top. Soon blue tits all over Britain had picked up this tip! It's as if the information passed along instantaneously once enough of them learned how to break the seals. Blue tits are known to congregate in large flocks compared to other species and this allows them to communicate adaptive ideas extremely quickly.

AGGRESSIVE COMPETITION

As a young, litigation lawyer, I took great pride when our managing partner referred to me as a 'Rotweiller in court' to our opponents. I was certain this helped me become successful. So I was taken aback when I learned that in many recent studies the results suggest the *less* competitive one feels the more one will succeed. In his enlightening book, *No contest: The Case Against Competition*, Alfie Kohn found compelling evidence that competition is toxic, not only to the job, but also to the soul. When we are working in a competitive environment we can become blocked emotionally. He shows us how competition causes the following:

- Poisons relationships
- Makes us suspicious, hostile and envious
- Destroys our self esteem
- Creates anxiety and the need for approval
- Is inefficient
- Undermines genuine love of learning by focusing on external gain
- Kills curiosity

He argues that competition is aggression. So what is the alternative?

- Co-operation and partnership
- An atmosphere of co-creation. We can work together to come up with fresh ideas. No one has to do it alone – and what a relief that can be!

Have you noticed that when you feel deeply, either the excitement of joy, or the sadness of sorrow, you immediately become more open and alive? Even if we are moved just a bit, we have transcended our normal, routine physical concerns. When we are under pressure, our hearts and minds are constricted and we can't see beyond our physical needs and desires. Our sensitivity to spiritual arousal is blocked, our capacity for higher awareness is limited and we focus on mundane things.

In business terms, a harmonious economic interaction is called the 'meeting of minds' or 'goodwill' and is the basis of all contracts. We sense that we can't be completely dominated by the mundane forces of corporate life. We want our intellectual perceptions to come around to the perspective of the heart, so what better place to start than with our fellow colleagues?

Sincerity is the essence of the spiritual heart. But manipulation is the cloak of a clouded mind that is driven by ego. This includes slyness, scheming and under-handed attacks on colleagues. We can learn a lot from small children – their behaviour has a total absence of artificiality. A child's very soul is expressed in each of his activities. He is transparent. His soul shines in everything he does. Imagine what it would be like if we retained that state into adulthood. How would you feel if you could be like that at work?

A 'spiritual relationship' with others is not necessarily one in which we are smiling saints all the time. We are not here to audition one another, put others on trial or use them to gratify our needs. We are not here to fix, change or belittle another person. We are here to support each other and to grow from this experience. It is easy to find fault with your fellow workers and get irritated when they do not see things your way. Sometimes this tension builds up leading to frosty encounters at the coffee machine.

Also, life mirrors what is going on inside you. If you feel challenged by others all the time, decide instead to focus on behaviours that show the best of human nature. If you must dwell on the factors and the people that annoy you, do so metaphorically from a mountain top. Look down from above and be stunned that nature has deprived so many people of a natural overview, and this has created so many potentially awkward situations. Stay high. Commit to seeing every little thing in your workplace as a potentially spiritually enlightening experience.

THE POWER OF COMPASSIONATE PRAYER

Most of us find ourselves addressing a Higher Power in times of great stress and trauma. Even confirmed atheists may find themselves on their knees with hands clasped together when things are really bad and they see no other option. What really happens if we are honest is a form of begging with a few desperate promises.

Though they are often answered, there are much more powerful ways of praying. How many of us take the time to offer a prayer of thanks and gratitude every time things are going well? When the universe sends you something you like acknowledging that invites more of the same into your life.

Praying out of gratitude is very powerful, but most powerful of all is praying on behalf of others. How many of us routinely pray for others, especially others who are not in our immediate circle of family and close friends? Not only does such prayer benefit you and those you are praying for in subtle ways through healing vibrations, it also reminds you that we are all connected. If you do this regularly, you will find it much harder to fall prey to the dog-eat-dog, cutthroat mentality. The highest form and finest energy we can work with is *unconditional love*.

- One female client who is a director of a major PR company has the practice of praying for each member of her staff. She feels this is an outgrowth of her own spirituality.

- Another Hindu client has a statue of Lord Ganesh in his office who is the remover of any obstacles. He does a short prayer before he begins any important work or contracts.

- A senior partner of a well known accountancy firm always does a silent prayer before he starts a meeting and asks that the outcome is beneficial to all attending.

- I often use my commute time for my daily meditation and prayers - to pray for my clients' well-being and happiness. This is my spiritual gift to others.

LAUGHTER – THE UNIVERSAL PICK-ME-UP

Many of us are very serious at work. Often the first thing to go in the workplace is the very thing that helps us keep things in perspective: our sense of humour! What is it about humour that makes life easier to live? What is the connection between humour and health, vitality and the ability to go the extra mile?

Work is a place where we have been taught to rely on our heads – our intellects. We constantly think things through and reason things out. Often, in order for us to do this successfully we have to put aside what's going on in our bodies. We ignore what we're feeling and what our instincts are telling us. We push down and push away the information that the body carries so that we can make 'reasonable', 'logical' and 'rational' choices based on our analysis. Yet it is now well established that self-awareness and recognising a feeling as it happens is the cornerstone of emotional intelligence.

Think of the last time you laughed until you cried. Remember how your heart felt. Remember how your muscles tightened and caused your body posture to shift and your presence to take on a whole new shape? Laughter decreases levels of the stress hormone cortisol and is increasingly being recognised as a powerful form of therapy. Laughter centres are appearing all over the globe.

However, it is worth paying attention to the kind of humour that pervades your workplace. Are things easy and light? Or is your humour dark, often dismissive of someone or something? Is the humour dis-empowering and cynical? Do you shroud nasty comments aimed to hurt others with the words: "Can't you take a joke?"

In order for light-hearted humour to be present in the workplace there has to be a sense of safety and acceptance: that it's okay to say what's on your mind and to say things that fly in the face of the status quo. It's not about being a threat, but about creating and contributing and making a difference. Humour makes it easier for us to handle harsh truths. When we're able to laugh at ourselves, we're drawing upon our courage. It also inspires others to let go of their masks and practice truth.

Start to have fun at work with your peers. Go ahead – share a joke and a laugh! Once my colleague and I were marooned in the office until the small hours on Christmas Eve. Beavering away under a mountain of papers to complete a deal was not our idea of yuletide fun! It was a sight to behold with our smudged make-up, oil tanker spillage hair, wearing slippers with our dark suits and sipping left over champagne from the Christmas party straight from the bottle! What cheered me up was her jovial interjections like, *"I feel like we're in the world's worst reality show here but this is going to make a great story when it's all over."* It reminds you that the facts of any situation are always changing and as soon as you alter the way you see things, you begin to change reality. Humour connects you to a sense of optimism. You can come up with a more empowering script than, *"God I hate this job!"*

People who enjoy their life work harder, make more money and have more confidence in themselves. They have more friends and are far healthier than those people who worry constantly. Celebrations spontaneously arise when people feel connected. You see that in offices where a team member is honoured on their birthday with a gift or when a boss decides to take his junior out for a celebratory drink for passing tough professional exams.

There's no doubt that everyday life can be absurd and that the universe has a sense of humour. In Hinduism, the sacred symbol *Om* is said to be the sound of the universe laughing. Greet each day with a sense of awe and an expectation of wonderful things. Before too long you'll be seeing magic and joy, instead of stress and heartache. Smile when you see someone, welcome a new employee and compliment a colleague on their work.

Whether you are at work, at home or on holiday your attitude about your life defines how your life unfolds. It is *how* you do your work and connect with people that really matters. From a spiritual perspective, a successful life is one in which you radiate more good than bad vibrations or energy. Make a choice today to live the fullest life possible - filled with friends and enjoyable work. The world will then be a better place for all of us. j

---

REFLECT

Starting today see the world in a different light. Be creative. Visualise difficult situations as if they are a cartoon with funny characters. See the humour in things. Put a smile on your face, learn to see the beauty all around and take a deep breath. Instead of criticising someone count to 10 when frustrated and take a walk instead of clenching your teeth. Think about how our light can shine brightly together, creating even greater light.

A blessing is an expression of thanks or a prayer. I see it as a transfer of energy which helps others to fulfil their potential. It is an act of service. A blessing should come straight from your heart, with sincerity and we can do this by deliberately going into the most loving mood of which we are capable. This may seem really hard sometimes, but we are all equipped to do it if we try!

You can bless a difficult situation, even if the person involved may not be receptive to your efforts. There may be

---

something that touches your heart and evokes compassion. For me it is babies and so if someone upsets me I imagine them as a vulnerable baby or a child full of innocence, before I am able to do a heartfelt blessing. Blessing the situation helps you to understand and discover the good and the lessons in the experience. It allows us to move with grace and humility and rise above what seems negative.

A blessing is a natural act that we can all do and is not just restricted to priests or gurus. The most common way is to use your hands as a conduit for this benevolent energy, but if you feel shy or embarrassed then do a silent blessing in your mind. Don't forget to switch on a huge inner smile and feel the lovely, vibrant change in your body.

When you are at work silently offer the person on your left and right an appropriate short blessing. Imagine your silent words creating a healing light energy around them which connects to your own energy level and strengthens your working relationship with them. Breathe gratitude and acceptance into the moment – make it real and see the difference.

Team Play

Serve To Lead

"The leader shows that style is no substitute for substance… that creating an impression is not more potent than acting from one's centre."

LAO TZU, CHINESE PHILOSOPHER, 6TH CENTURY B.C.

Imagine the Dalai Lama in a smart saffron coloured cotton suit with his fingers touching in a triangle shape, his elbows leaning on the Indian teak round table in the boardroom. He is noted for his sharp business mind and ranked as the most influential person in the business world. He is smiling and his presence brims with enthusiasm as he begins to pour you some green tea in a delicate china cup, eager to hear from you. You are surprised at how relaxed he is and wonder how such a heavyweight tycoon has not only made time for you but appears to show faith in what you are about to say, even before you say it! There is none of the usual painful trepidation before a sales pitch to the head honcho. This makes you feel good inside and confident that you will be heard with an open mind.

Forget the macho pin stripe image of a hurried leader bellowing, "you're fired!" This leader wants to know how you are and what he can do for you. His strength lies in his incredible ability to inspire others to greatness.

What if this far-fetched scenario were possible? Could you be inspired by such a leader or would you find it difficult to take him seriously? Think about how you answered the latter question and what it reveals about your expectations of what a leader should be like.

The word 'leadership' is an old English word that actually means to go first. The consciousness of the leader has a significant impact on the consciousness of the organisation. What trail of scent would you leave behind as a leader?

Simon Watkins writes in *The Mail On Sunday*: *"Words such as ethics and morality would not frighten Stephen Green. Although he heads the world's biggest non-state run bank, the chairman of HSBC is also an ordained Anglican priest. HSBC has faced calls from activist shareholders to cut and run from its troubled US Household business, which is running massive losses. Legally the bank could walk away, effectively putting Household into administration leaving creditors to carry the losses. To Green, that is unthinkable. 'This all points to something more profound about market ethics. Our word is our bond and the idea that you can play fast and loose with that is immoral. I genuinely believe one of the biggest issues is that we must change the culture.' In his 1996 book Serving God? Serving Mammon? he warns that those working in financial markets risk becoming 'obsessed with wealth and power' and in danger of 'selling one's soul'. He concludes that Christianity and banking are not automatically incompatible. 'The markets, flawed as they are like every other human structure, can be used to contribute to human development. Being there also creates opportunities – to show an integrity that loves others as ourselves and treats them as ends rather than means'."*[1]

---

[1] April 5th 2009 The Mail on Sunday 'High priest of HSBC and a Lesson the World Will Not Forget' by Simon Watkins

If we are going to change the system we need courageous individuals to risk liberating their minds from the mechanistic thinking of the 'command and control' ways of running a company. *"You can't transform a group structure without having the leadership go through some sort of transformation,"* says Richard Barrett, author of *Liberating the Corporate Soul.*

Vision means seeing beyond the obvious – seeing the unseen. Visionaries see a vision of what can be, of possibilities beyond the status quo and articulate them with great clarity. They then follow their vision in spite of obstacles and non-believers.

A visionary leader is good with actions as well as words and so can manifest his vision. Muhammad Yunis, winner of the 2006 Nobel Peace Prize and founder of the Grameen Bank is one of the originators of micro-financing. Rather than holding onto the dis-empowering story that there will always be poverty, he envisioned helping women by investing in their enterprises. He was watering the seeds of abundance they already possessed. What he discovered is that despite abject poverty, the women who benefit from the small loans pay them back at a rate of nearly 100 percent. They use their money not only to help themselves and their children but to employ other women as well.

A visionary leader can stand strong and secure in the presence of others. They are not shaken, threatened or jealous of other people's power. In fact they honour and welcome the strengths of others.

I have witnessed these amazing qualities in one of my clients, who is a director of a multi-national food company. She lives by her commitment to be truthful. She prefers to be straightforward. Sometimes she has failed to deliver on time, but she tells the customers exactly how it is and they still remain loyal. Lies or games are of no interest to her, but she's not easy to fool. She is experienced in the ways of the world and can size up a situation very quickly. I believe she is a great leader – she understands human mistakes and weaknesses but does not condemn them. She knows when cow manure is being thrown around and finds constructive ways to handle internal conflicts. She has a steady and even temperament that adds an element of stability to any situation. One thing for sure is that she likes a good laugh and is refreshing in her spirit and lack of pretence. She encourages her staff in their goals and aspirations and lends support when needed. One of her staff members said to me that: *"She really cares for us sincerely – we know this because she gives her time generously and we find her approachable."*

Ken Blanchard, Bill Hybels and Phil Hodges describe the term 'servant leader' in *Leadership by the Book: Tools To Transform Your Workplace*. They maintain that leaders who are servants first will assume leadership only if they see it as the best way they can serve. They are 'called' to lead rather than driven, because they naturally want to be helpful. They use their talents and abilities for the greater good of the organisation.

The authors use Jesus Christ as a true model and symbol of the servant leader as he came to earth to serve and *not* to be served. Unlike the kings of the past, he did not rally his people to fight in bloody battles and die for him. He died for his people: the ultimate sacrifice for the greater good.

This is a model radically different from the prevailing reality in the corporate world. It is not service driven by ego, nor by the 'status syndrome' where we are always trying to get others to serve us. The servant leader asks, 'what can I do for *you*?' People do not normally associate business with generosity and kindness, because business is seen to be only a tool to make money.

The biggest debilitating compulsion in the corporate world today is to automatically consider every question from the point of view of, 'What's in it for me?' The paramount aim of servant leaders is the interests of those they lead. Personal power, money or recognition is never the focus. Servant leaders get great personal satisfaction from watching others grow and develop their skills.

Servant leaders value and demonstrate democracy and inclusiveness by listening and creating empowering relationships. The work gets done by inspiring workers with vision and by example, rather than dominating them. This approach creates 'power with' rather than 'power over' – a co-operative blend of leadership and empowered equality.

When we have a leader who thinks everyone is there to serve him and treats them with a 'hired hands' attitude, thinking only about his own prosperity, what do we feel about him? Contrast this with what happens when we are led by someone who genuinely cares about us and has our best interests in mind and at heart. We are very likely to *exceed expectations.* True leaders know where the credit belongs when the applause comes.

This sort of genuine humility does not rule out confidence. In fact it creates a new type of boldness.

Servant leaders educate and coach rather than simply direct. They inspire responsibility rather than create dependency and they assume that people already have the potential wisdom and creativity within them and their task is to draw this out. Servant leaders help others to develop self-confidence and a sense of self-worth. As the ancient Chinese sage Lao Tzu said *"Leadership is best when the people say, 'We have done this ourselves!'"*

DOING WELL BY DOING GOOD

Spiritual values that could be widely embraced in business include integrity, honesty, accountability, loyalty, quality, co-operation, intuition, trust, respect, equality and service.

A commitment to values is an outstanding characteristic of all visionary leaders who embody a sense of personal integrity and radiate energy, vitality and confidence. More self-aware and reflective than others, such visionary leaders follow and lead from an inner conviction. Mahatma Gandhi is a prime example of someone committed to his core values, as he freed India by appealing to the moral conscience of Britain and using 'satyagraha' or non-violent action to usurp the immorality of the British Empire.

In 1989, two professors of the Stanford Business School, Dr James Collins and Dr Jerry Porras, analysed over 100 successful executives with whom they worked. Their conclusion reflected that the ingredients common to each were a sense of *purpose, mission and vision.* They had a sense of destiny that gave them a compelling future to aspire to.

This is perhaps a good time to write down your own core principles and values. This exercise may be a useful moment of insight for you. You will learn something about yourself, particularly what drives you. Take a few minutes now to think about this. The key is to reflect deeply and write out your personal mission statement. For it to be effective try to read it regularly.

Why is this so important? As James Callaghan, former Prime Minister of Britain stated: *"In my judgment, a leader should have a core philosophy and belief against which he can judge the important issues as they arise. Unless he has that bedrock to fall back on, the unexpected storms that blow up will toss him about like a cork. Without such a foundation, a leader may be able to survive, but he won't be a leader in the sense that I use the term."*

You will find that identifying your core principles and values will give you a sense of purpose and meaning. To give you an example, here is my work value statement:

To inspire and empower people to live their highest vision in a context of joy and spiritual growth.

By writing it down and reading it every day I have developed a commitment to it. So this means I will always know how I will act in any given situation. The result of such a deep commitment to one's values is *personal power*. It is an invigorating force that fills you up and lends you the courage to be great.

This power comes not from the core values alone, but from the strength of one's commitment to them. It takes personal dedication and personal reminders. Since we are in such a busy world, we are often so task-focused that we forget our inner core values that drive us. The challenge is to constantly keep reaching within ourselves, pulling out our values and staying true to them. Unless people do that their spirituality will not take root. It's not really magic – it's about transformation using post-it notes and pocket books if that is what it takes!

On a deeper level, true power always comes from the Divine. It passes through us and then flows out into the world. When we understand this relationship we are blessed because this flow brings with it a tremendous feeling of expansion and fulfilment. We feel we can accomplish anything. Problems develop when we forget we are not the source of this power, only its conduit. Power should not intoxicate us to obscure our good sense and we must use it wisely.

This list outlines some commonly held values. Which ones are important to you?

Variety	Creativity	Challenge
Freedom	Reputation	Being the best
Power	Status	Independence
Intellect	Security	Respect
Spirituality	Intimacy	Family bonds
Integrity	Commitment	Trust

As an extension of the above exercise now think about aligning all your actions and behaviour to your core values. The secret to a successful career is realising that it is not separate from the rest of your life, but an extension of your inner self.

Once when Mahatma Gandhi was speaking in England, he held a group of people spellbound for several hours without any preparation and in a relatively uncomfortable environment. The crowds were enthralled by what this remarkable man had to say. Reporters were amazed that he was able to speak so convincingly without any notes. His secretary, Mahadev Desai explained: *"What Gandhi thinks, he feels; what he says, and what he does are all the same. He does not need notes."* He was all lined up and at one with himself and his core values.

Once we line up our deep commitment to our core values with our actions we have integrity. You don't have to wait for your moment of greatness. Rosa Parks by the time she refused to give up her seat on an Alabama bus to a white person in 1955, she'd already been involved in the struggle for civil rights for years. She lived her life in alignment with her deepest values, so when she needed courage, it was there for her. Acting out of integrity did not take enormous effort, for it was her established habit.

HOW LINED UP ARE YOU WITH YOUR CORE VALUES?

When I walked away from a profession I'd served for over a decade, I didn't think I had anything in common with people who take the bull by the horn and are true to themselves. But in fact, I actually did. It was a scary and very isolating walk off a cliff called 'security'. That was the only way I could be honest with myself. I was comfortably successful and didn't have to leave. Most days I liked the paycheque that funded my bellini nights out, my ever increasing fondness for Jimmy Choos and having my very own PA who booked my spa weekends for me. Yet there was something missing and things just began to get at me. Complacency set in and I felt I needed more of a challenge. I didn't feel I was running away from anything, it was more like moving towards a new fulfilling life. I needed to test my mettle as a soloist building my own consultancy and branding. This thought excited me like no other and just stayed with me day and night.

I wanted to experience the emotions that Michelangelo once did as he created his sculptures from his imagination. I wanted to feel my work with that kind of rare, magical intensity. Such lofty aspirations! Looking back I have no regrets. The journey has been awesome as I have had the opportunity to do the most challenging, creative and karmic work since then. To me, success is also knowing that I have on a deeper level, energetically helped humankind and the earth. When you belong nowhere you begin to question who exactly you are when you leave. Quite unexpectedly my commitment to my core values carried me forward to the inner work of personal and spiritual growth. Each of us at some point in our lives takes a stand alone. But the moment we do, we tend to attract supportive kindred spirits who have also taken those brave steps.

True character is not being worried about being popular – it's about doing what is right, not what is necessarily convenient. When you put effort into aligning your actions with your core values this results in trust. People sense when you are acting out of deeper values and you will find they are more willing to follow your ideas, suggestions and contributions to your organisation. Without it they feel something isn't quite right and may sense manipulation and only follow you grudgingly, if at all.

Notice how great visionaries stir up energy in others – they are not running around all over the place. Their personal power is like an invisible force around them that inspires others to get things done. This aura makes them attractive and like a magnet they draw the right people and circumstances that lead to success.

If we change our values to suit the occasion or our current mood, it is like having no anchor and we are at risk of sinking. However, if we self-correct our behaviours to match our core values this usually *increases trust.* Visionary leaders can apologise and rectify their behaviour as soon as they realise that their values and behaviour are out of sync. They do this quickly – they do not dwell on it or bend their values to fit in with impulsive actions or thoughtless behaviours. In the words of Dee Groberg, founding vice president of the International Covey Leadership Center: *"It takes courage to... self-correct when you are wrong. Because it is difficult, it offers an opportunity for greatness."*

Those leaders that we admire and look up to have all 'failed' at some point in their lives and they continue to do so. They too have doubts to overcome, demons to face and disappointments to make peace with. We tend to look to heroes as examples of perfection and become disappointed if we learn they are human, like us. We don't want to hear that Martin Luther King Jr had extramarital affairs or that John Lennon wrote all we need is love but barely had a relationship with his oldest son. I was deeply upset for weeks when someone told me that Mahatma Gandhi who believed in non-violence used to beat his wife. Whether this is true or not their flaws do not erase their good work and nor should our weaknesses incapacitate us from courageous action. All of us can do great things even if we tend to be irritable, angry or even arrogant. Release your need to be perfect. It's not going to happen.

PULLING THE PEOPLE LEVER

"As we look ahead into the next century, leaders will be those who empower others."

BILL GATES, BUSINESS MAGNATE

Influence is about empowerment – and not just your empowerment. Many people feel dis-empowered and disengaged at work because they lack influence. Remember the last time you heard a salesperson say: "I can't do anything about that – it's not part of my job. You need to write to our head office." The servant leader would say, "I totally understand how you feel. What you need to do is to take the complaint to X. Here is her direct number. I'm going to call her now to brief her." How different would that make you feel?

Anyone can be influential, not just people in positions of power. You might help someone feel more confident so they can handle a complex matter or teach them a new skill. *A candle loses nothing by lighting another candle.*

Become aware of the many possibilities you have for influencing others and that will help you become more aware of your own value. Influence is about offering others something that they will be glad to receive – whether that is practical help, emotional support or constructive criticism. Influence in this sense is a valuable currency increasing the value of the organisation as a whole.

IMPOSTOR SYNDROME

In all walks of life there are leaders who believe they do not deserve their success. It has become so prevalent that psychologists have invented a new term for it: 'neurotic imposture'. Writing in a 2005 article in *The Guardian,* Insead professor of leadership Manfred Kets de Vries said: *"To some extent, of course, we are all impostors. Displaying a facade is part and parcel of the human condition. But neurotic impostors feel more fraudulent and alone than other people do. Because they view themselves as charlatans, their success is worse than meaningless: it is a burden. 'Bluffing' their way through life (as they see it), they are haunted by the constant fear of exposure. With every success, they think: 'I was lucky this time, but will my luck hold? When will people discover that I'm not up to the job?'"*

A neurotic impostor is a perfectionist who sets impossible goals; in other words, who sets him or herself up for failure. For many, the root of the problem is the fear that success will cost them too dearly; often, specifically, the fear that family, friends and others will continue to like them much better if they remain 'small'. The mindset can lead to self-destructive behaviour which, ironically, often brings about the very failure that keeps such people awake at night.

Not everyone who carries around this heavy psychological burden is a leader, but in my personal experience leaders are especially prone to it. One of the most dangerous side effects of neurotic imposture is its possible effects on decision-making. Leaders who feel like impostors are afraid to trust their own judgment. Their overly cautious kind of leadership can easily spread across a corporate culture and cast a shadow over the whole company.

A person's strengths are also her weaknesses and neurotic imposture is the flip side of leadership; in fact, it is a rare leader who does not suffer from it to some extent, at some time during their careers. Therefore, it is important for leaders to be on the lookout for it in themselves and their subordinates. Encourage a culture where open, honest feedback – including constructive criticism – is freely given and warmly welcomed. Always be sure to give praise where it's due and make sure your staff know that making mistakes (and learning from them!) is part of a successful business culture.

RECAP

To engage the heart at work is:

1. To see people as people, not as employees.
2. To assume an intention of good will on their part.
3. To recognise a job well done, not just with money but also with a genuine appreciation. The 'you get your thanks in your pay cheque' attitude produces cynicism and resentment in workers.
4. To remember that people are creative and capable. It is to believe in them, not just the numbers.

To engage the soul at work is to realise listening to people and responding to them is not a waste of time. Next time a colleague comes to see you try making a point of looking up and pushing your chair back from your desk: the message you give is that you have time for them and give them your full attention. They will feel at ease so they can tell you what they want to say.

REFLECT

Think back for a few moments on your last week at work. Was there something you saw beyond the ordinary and mundane? Did you follow your values? Ask yourself:

1. Am I a positive force in this office?
- Do I help people feel good about themselves or am I always pulling them down? See what happens when you act as if your actions really make a difference to those in your office.
- If I were the most important leader in this office, what would I be doing?

2. Think about empowering others. It doesn't matter if others become more successful than you. What is important is that you define and value your own personal vision of success.

3. Identify someone you admire who is a leader in your work, family or community:
- What skills or attitude do they demonstrate that you particularly like?
- Which of these skills do you possess or could you develop?
- What steps will you take over the next month to develop these skills?

4. Write your own acceptance speech for a leadership award. Read it out loud in front of an imaginary audience.

5. Say a thank you blessing to all the mentors and role models you have in your life. Remind yourself that all the wisdom, courage, integrity and strength of your mentors lies within you too.

Entrepreneurs Make A Difference

"In terms of power and influence, you can forget the church, forget politics. There is no more powerful institution in society than business – I believe it is now more important than ever before for business to assume a moral leadership. The business of business should not be about money, it should be about responsibility. It should be about public good, not private greed."

ANITA RODDICK, FOUNDER OF THE BODY SHOP

The universe always supports our integrity. This is why spiritual companies are more functional than unethical ones. Sure, you can run a profitable business with the ethics of a rogue. But you will always have to watch your back, fend off investigations and never know when the dodgy deeds will catch up with you. You can also run a profitable business with the state-of-the-art spiritual agenda, bask in the goodwill of your raving clients, enjoy the harmony at work and earn a great public image. Spirituality is good for you and good for business.

A corporate culture that, for example, even tacitly permits the production of medication with seriously debilitating side effects, needs to be changed. The same can be said for a school which does not endeavour to educate every student. In these cases we must discern what to change and seek the courage to change it. If you are in the lucky position of running your own business you are free to mould and shape that entity in any way you want. However, employees at all levels of an organisation have the power to influence.

Hindu tradition spells out the consequences of doing harm with *Karma*, the universal law of cause and effect. What goes around, comes around. The only uncertainty is the precise form the effect will take and how soon it will manifest in your life. So why not start playing our part in bringing about that better world rather than devoting our energy to finding ways of getting away with things. Personally, I would love to live in a world where people refrain from doing things not because they're afraid they'll get caught, but simply because they are wrong.

Start to make choices that go beyond a simple material transaction. For example, if you are considering placing an advertisement in a journal, consider whether you want to be identified with the ethos of that particular publication. If you are in PR, check that what you are promoting on behalf of your clients is in line with your ethics. What impact is your business having on the environment and what choices can you make to improve this picture? It may be something as simple as being less wasteful. Discern your role in a greater framework and not only the monetary cost to you. When choosing your dentist, doctor, accountant, lawyer, hairdresser and so on, ascertain whether they share your personal values. Remember you have a choice to work with people who have the same values as you and can bring out the best in you.

It is inspiring to observe that some business leaders can see past personal gain and recognise that our businesses must stand for something beyond profit. A prime example is Body Shop founder Dame Anita Roddick whose legacy of addressing health and environmental problems, as well as poverty in the Developing World, through innovative strategies changed the face of business. Products were made of non-polluting ingredients manufactured without cruelty to animals and shops were opened in poor areas to provide employment and return profit to the community.

Corporate social responsibility – also referred to, increasingly, as 'sustainability' – has been around for some time. The notion really began to take off in the early 1990s as increasing concern about the environment – especially climate change. With much of the world now in recession, the coming years will demonstrate whether CSR really has been embraced by corporations or whether it is – as some say – simply a marketing ploy designed to put a positive spin on their reputation.

Roger Trapp writes in *The Independent*: *"Recent research has produced hard evidence to show that responsible businesses can still succeed according to traditional criteria. Business in the Community has carried out research that shows that companies consistently running their business according to responsible principles outperformed the FTSE 350 on total shareholder return between 2002 and 2007 by between 3.3 per cent and 7.7 per cent per year. Businesses have also pointed to improvements in their reputations as a result of having been seen to do 'good things'. Customers trust them, while staff feel good about their work."*[2]

---

[2] *The Independent* 10th March 2009 'Corporate Social Responsibility is Vital for Business Survival' by Roger Trapp

Bill Gates, founder of Microsoft and now a major philanthropist, launched his idea of *"creative capitalism"* as *"a way to make the aspects of capitalism that serve wealthier people serve poorer people as well"*. One development, already under way, is the social business – an enterprise set up specifically to deal with certain issues. Examples include People Tree, a fashion company that sells distinctive garments in British and Japanese high streets through forging sustainable partnerships with Fair Trade and organic producers in developing countries; and Divine Chocolate, which gives cocoa farmers in Ghana direct access to the mainstream chocolate market in the UK and elsewhere. Both organisations are blossoming.

THE EARTH HOUSEHOLD

There are now over six billion of us on this planet and whilst we are more culturally fragmented, we are also more interconnected. Everything is both global and local – *everywhere*. The body of our planet is a living organism (called 'gaia' by the ancients) and all economic interactions from the individual to the international take place within this moving energy. If circulation through the system is blocked through manipulation, hoarding or fraud, then all parts of the organisation suffer. When there is free circulation of goods, resources and services throughout the gaia, nourishing all parts of the system, then the whole flourishes.

Economics literally means 'earth household'. If we care for the planetary economy as we would our own household, we can see that it must work for all members or it will not work in the long term. Just as we wouldn't tear our house apart to make a fire to keep warm or dump nuclear waste in our gardens, so we must respect the larger household as our own. We must do right and understand the effect of our actions on future generations who will inhabit the earth. Let's stop being a real pain in the ass for our planet!

We scramble to find quick solutions which can be futile and painfully expensive. Panicking and trying to create material security because we fear any sort of sacrifice of our material comfort has a high cost. Even on a collective level we seem to go for a quick fix with minimal effort. In the past several years, Ecuador has lost 40 per cent of its rain forests due to drilling for oil to feed the insatiable western appetite for fossil fuels. Yet they only harvested enough oil to fuel America for two weeks. Are you taking any shortcuts in your business that you think will solve all your problems? Consider at what real cost...

We are the only species that makes unusable waste; the animal kingdom only makes things that can be used by others. We need to pay attention to Mother Nature – she has got it perfectly in order. I was so heartened to learn that many scientists want to create ingenious products with this in mind. A company has designed an ice cream wrapper that degrades within hours. In an article by Elisabeth Debold for the March 2005 issue of *What Is Enlightenment* magazine, Dr Michael Braungart of McDonough Braungart Design Chemistry says: *"But the nice thing is that it is not just biodegradable. That's the minimum. Because the ice-cream packaging contains seeds from rare plants, by throwing it away, you're supporting biodiversity like every songbird does"*. Man-made waste becomes a nutrient – how remarkable!

Yet humanity as a whole still has a long way to travel up this particular learning curve. Bound by restrictive legislation, many western companies go to countries like

China to produce low quality products much more cheaply with lower environmental standards. These products – for example toys made out of plasticizers that give off sterility-causing gases when children chew on them – are true weapons of mass destruction.

The constant rush to market new products has transformed the quality of our lives. Sony launches three new products per hour and 70% of Hewlett Packard's revenue comes from products that didn't exist last year. Such is the power of the corporate juggernaut. At the same time this demand, propelled by the profit motive, has caused atrocious damage to this planet and its inhabitants.

Debold highlights that the biggest soft drinks companies are under scrutiny from watchdog organisations for water pollution and for creating 'opportunity' from water scarcity. In its Coca-Cola profile the Polaris Institute quotes from the company's 1993 annual report: *"All of us in the Coca-Cola family wake up each morning knowing that every single one of the world's 5.6 billion people will get thirsty that day. If we make it impossible for these 5.6 billion people to escape Coca-Cola, then we assure our future success for many years to come. Doing anything less is not an option."*

Further, Brian Bacon of the Oxford Leadership Academy is quoted as saying: *"Short-term profit drives large corporations to buy up small companies and inventions that 'threaten' them with potentially costly change – and then do nothing with the inventions themselves. It's the reason Pfizer, which has substantial community service programs, invests little or nothing in attempting to cure simple diseases that kill millions worldwide, like malaria and tuberculosis, but will invest an enormous amount researching baldness because they can make a killing by selling its 'cure' to the affluent."*

Well-intentioned business leaders can find they are prevented from being morally responsible. Bob Hinckley was formerly a partner at the prestigious law firm Skadden Arps, but took a break from his practice after realising the painful truth of this. *"I am suggesting that the corporate law be changed to say: 'The duty of directors henceforth shall be to make money for the shareholders but not at the expense of the environment, human rights, public health and safety, dignity of employees, and the welfare of the communities in which the company operates'."* Hinckley points out that companies are capable of side-stepping the legal system through well-financed lobbying to create the rules they are happy with. Sometimes they aggressively flout the law; because they have the funds to engage in long legal battles which they can afford to lose.

A strong lobby is needed for the radical change Hinckley proposes, whereby companies will be accountable for their effects on the environment and committed to find better ways to innovate in line with nature. We need to shift our consciousness away from the mechanistic mindset that invented the company. It is this mindset that created our sense of separation from each other.

Today the haves and the have-nots are brushing shoulders throughout the globe and a new pressure is building up. What would it take to stop the destructiveness of these gargantuan entities? Remember, organisations don't change – people do. The question is, is there the willingness?

Many of today's companies are morally and creatively asleep. But you and I can wake them. Imagine what it would be like to go to work each morning for a company that really put consumers first and saw your passions and your idealism as what will take you forward to success. By reinventing capitalism and infusing our own souls into the machine, we can raise the stakes for human possibility.

We know that many companies have amassed resources and power that rival those of certain third-world nations. That is why big business can do so much – in fact I'd say that *business is the most powerful force on this planet.*

SO YOU THINK IT WON'T PAY TO BE NICE?

In their 1997 book *Built to Last*, James Collins and Jerry Porras identified eighteen visionary companies that, between 1926 and 1990, achieved a growth in shareholder value 15 times greater than the general market. Their research shows that contrary to business school doctrine, maximising shareholder wealth was not the main driving force of these visionary companies.

They had tended to pursue a cluster of objectives, of which making money was only one - and not necessarily the primary one. Visionary companies had objectives that transcended purely economic considerations. The majority of their objectives (44%) concerned well-being and only 20% concerned corporate fitness. Surprisingly, only 6% of the objectives mentioned corporate survival (profits or shareholder value). Some of the more inspiring statements adopted by these companies were:

*"We are in the business of preserving
and improving human life."*

"People are the source of our strength."

"Improving the quality of life through technology and innovation."

"People are number one — treat them well, expect a lot, and the rest will follow."

US retailer Whole Foods is a shining example of ethical entrepreneurship. Says co-president Walter Robb: *"We're not retailers who have a mission – we're missionaries who retail. At the very heart and soul of Whole Foods is the mission. We're here to make a real difference in people's health and well-being, in the health and well being of the planet, and in creating a workplace based on love and respect."* Robb adds that the company is, *"willing to take steps to change things. We've got to take concrete steps to show not only our own team members, but also the world, that we are serious about our principles."*

For example, the company stopped selling sea bass, one of its top-selling fish, when it discovered it was not being fished in a sustainable manner. Despite an explicit policy of putting customers and staff before shareholders, the company has delivered a 25% compounded annual growth rate. *"Our return on invested capital is north of thirty-five percent,"* says Robb. *"Those are some of the strongest numbers in the history of food retailing."*

Austrian philosopher Rudolf Steiner coined the term 'associative economics'. He said that unless you could link the consumer, the producer and the distributor of the services into the same organisation, you would always have false economics that would pit those different parties against each other in a win-lose situation. *"Whereas if you create [...] structures designed to optimise the whole – all three parts – then you can do things that are miraculous, because you can move money around for the benefit of the whole as opposed to the benefit of only one part."*

There is now a payment card, the Interra, which rewards the purchaser for supporting businesses that have holistic values and also takes a small payment off each transaction to donate to a cause the purchaser supports. Greg Stetenpohl, co-founder of the Interra Project says: *"We asked what could be a structure... that would allow the values of sustainability and cooperative activity to be built into whatever we do? What if we formed a membership that included both businesses and consumers? And what if we created a movement that could shift the flow of dollars toward those places in society that would do the most good?"*

Joseph Jaworski, founder of Generon Consulting, lawyer and entrepreneur, was deeply inspired by spiritual leader, Dadi Janki of the Brahma Kumaris organisation, to do all that he possibly could to make a difference. His approach is unique. He brings together a group of individuals who represent a microcosm of the whole system. In the child nutrition program for instance, this group might include a mother in a village, local clerics, program officers from CARE as well as local and international business people involved in the food industry.

They start with the premise and honest acceptance that each of them has a different role in creating the system that is the problem. The aim is to get them totally engaged and committed to resolve the issue. The group learn about the real issues by actually going to those places around the world where the problem is most acute. They also engage in spiritual practices designed to take them into a deeper encounter with their purpose assisting them to become an instrument of powerful change. It just takes that one person to really care and be willing to make him or herself available for this process.

YOUR STAFF – THE LIFE FORCE OF YOUR BUSINESS

My years as an executive coach have taught me that employees so often feel unseen and unheard. What most people really want is to feel that they are a part of something. That it matters that they show up at work and give their best and that someone notices when they do, not just when they don't.

As Joe Tye wrote in his book, *Staying On Top: When The World's Upside Down: "Spirituality is a taboo subject in many organisations. In the long run, it is those organisations able to tap into the tremendous power of personal spiritual strength that will succeed in the marketplace."* When the individual is connected to the organisation, people become connected to something deeper – the desire to contribute to a larger purpose, to feel they are part of a greater whole. As this develops, we begin to openly acknowledge the need for others, to see our interdependence, and our desire to belong. Our tribal instinct awakens.

At any given time, around 20% of the workforce is looking for another job. And recruitment experts estimate that there will always be 60% open to offer. Apart from the damage to the business, the cost of departures is huge: between one-and-a-half and three times annual salary. It means large companies need a retention strategy rather than hastily adding a few 'bolt-ons' such as fun days or other events to boost morale. Companies need to develop a culture where all staff members are recognised, not only the key players.

Positive support and genuine acknowledgement can significantly improve performance and can make the difference between valued workers staying or leaving. Can your company afford to take the attitude that says, "We're too busy to deal with feelings"? Consider the time, productivity and money lost when problems escalate to litigation, or when we work with a simmering tension. It doesn't take a great deal of effort to start implementing spiritual standards into business. There isn't a large capital investment, it won't mean upgrading equipment, expanding the facilities, or creating a 'spirituality committee'. What it will take is:

- A willing management to be the *active* role models for the company.

- Creation of and publicity for a solid mission statement incorporating spiritual standards.

- Training of current and future employees in implementing the mission statement.

Okay, the last one does involve some expense, but the payoff can be tremendous. Look around at the companies that are doing the best during economic downturns. The most successful ones are those with high employee and customer loyalty, brought about by a strong management team that focuses on treating everyone fairly, offering win/win situations and setting the example of 'do unto others…' In other words, they are companies that embody a spiritual leadership model.

Vodafone has encouraged retention by offering staff a comprehensive menu of personal-development opportunities. Their Global Leadership programme, for example, puts talented managers through a development scheme that includes coaching, mentoring and participation in an MBA programme. Staff can transfer to other parts of the company to gain experience or study for professional qualifications. They are encouraged to submit their own development plans.

More and more companies are realising that to retain their life force they will need to cater to the higher needs of employees. Our old ways of doing business are falling away and being replaced by a growing recognition that the contribution itself is what matters – and you can contribute and have fun at the same time! We are learning that we do not need to do 'serious' things, seriously. That work can be play, and that play can be extremely productive and fun.

Sonia Stojanovic, in conjunction with McKinsey and Co., created a program that took more than 21,000 employees through personal development workshops. In addition to changing how people related to each other at work, the results were dramatic. ANZ Bank, previously the least preferred employer in Australian financial services, is now the employer of choice. Staff satisfaction increased by 35% in four years. The bank has won 'Australian Bank of the Year' for three years running and its stock price has more than doubled.

For Stojanovic, the secret of the success comes from tapping into the intrinsically human longing for meaning and wholeness: *"We're giving people hope – the hope to find meaning and to not compartmentalise their lives into home, work and self. We're inviting people to ask the questions: Why am I here? What is my contribution? How can the work I'm doing and the service I'm providing bring forth the best I can be in every moment? People really want to feel that what they are doing is being counted and is contributing to the success of the organisation as well as to the greater good. They are concerned about sustainability and future generations."*

REFLECT

1. If it were up to you, how would you create positive change at your workplace?

2. How would you begin to close the gulf between rich and poor?

3. What would you do to relieve our struggling ecosystem?

4. How is your company meeting your needs for a larger purpose? Is our consciousness more evolved outside the office than in it?

5. Think of ways to shift from a sales mentality to a service mentality. How would you behave?

6. For the next fortnight challenge yourself to strike the word 'I' from your vocabulary. Don't be surprised if you start to feel a bit uneasy – it's the ego that is shrinking and feeling sorry for itself!

And for those who run businesses:

1. Consider appointing a committee to explore how spirituality might impact your workplace, customers and productivity.

2. At your next staff meeting, ask people: "What's it really like for you to work here? What's it like when you wake up on Monday morning, and know that it's time to come back to work?" And then listen, not only with your ears, but also with your heart and soul.

3. Now ask yourself these questions:
- Are the people who work for me growing?

- Are they healthier or less healthy as a result of how they spend their working lives?

- Are they being paid a just and reasonable wage?

Part Two
Transformation

The Clearing

"It is only when we have the courage to face things without any self-deception or illusion that a light will develop out of events by which the path to success may be recognized."

I CHING OR THE BOOK OF CHANGES

Transformation is not a process, it is a *willingness*. It is now time to take an honest look at what's been holding you back and how you are going to move forward in your life. Through my coaching practice I have helped people from all rungs of the corporate ladder, from secretaries and graduate trainees to company directors and entrepreneurs. And over the years I've noticed the same obstacles coming up again and again for people.

The next three chapters take you through those obstacles on the path to career fulfilment and how to get over, under or around them. It is a distillation of the work I have done with my clients and you will find many real-life case studies showing how these principles have worked for people from all walks of life. I've divided the possible challenges you may be facing into three categories.

The first chapter of this section takes you through the ways you could be sabotaging yourself. Perhaps you are holding yourself back through limiting beliefs, counterproductive behaviours or poor time management. In the second section we turn our attention to your passion (or otherwise) for your current work. Finally, a look at the external factors of your working life: where you work, who you work with, who manages you and how happy (or otherwise) you are with all of this.

Personal growth is not always easy. In fact, it is one of our greatest challenges. Sometimes we must face our own ugliness. Often we have to become painfully aware of our unproductive values and patterns of behaviour before we are willing to give them up. We must realise the real cost of our unhelpful values and destructive behaviour.

You may notice aspects of yourself in the following examples. If you do notice some familiarity and feel disturbed, please do not be discouraged by this. It may feel bad – this is because you are no longer anaesthetised by being unaware of your behaviour. You are no longer distanced, through denial or disassociation, from your experience. You may be starting to see the truth about the games we all play from time to time. It takes courage – this is often called the path of the spiritual warrior – to endure the sharp pains of discovery rather than choose to take the dull pain of unconsciousness for the rest of your life. It is your choice.

Your task is to know what is really going on within you. We live in a planet of polarity – both negative and positive. Recognise both sides of your nature. Whatever is going on in your environment you are capable of handling and if you do not believe it, it is because you have not looked at your magnificence. The sign of a mature being is one who acknowledges the pull of different energy fields and makes the decision whether to follow a particular energy or not. They see *choices*.

To be a Master you must first be the master of your own life. You become aware that there are areas of your psyche that you have not looked at and these are often reflected as fears. It is like waking up, which means taking everything behind you that you have tried to hide and placing it in your vision. Your inner voice says, "I am ready. I want to know, so I can be harmless. I want to be harmless, because it is the only way to move in power on this planet". A true Master is one who has gone into all parts of his psyche, has found it all and turned away from nothing. All that is presented is accepted, no matter how seemingly dark. Life then takes on a very different meaning. Then no adversity is unwelcome and divine grace is always by your side. You slip into a space of gratitude, joy and acceptance.

Finish any unfinished business. Address your shadows and keep bringing them into the light and eventually they will dissipate. Hiding from yourself like this is fighting yourself. The minute you put out the call for change, new energy will start coming, and then you just need to receive it.

When you ask for assistance from anyone in looking at your shadows and fears, be wary of the relationship that turns into dependency. You must always maintain your personal power – only you have the real answers to your problems. No-one knows you better than yourself. The vibrational pattern of a true teacher is one who constantly turns you back on yourself to develop your own inner strengths and intuition.

In helping many of the clients you'll read about in the following pages, I use in part a coaching method known as the GROW model, which I'll now outline briefly.

- **Step 1 – Goal:** Coach and client agree on a specific aim, objective or outcome.

- **Step 2 – Reality:** Time is taken to look at the circumstances of the client's life, to check assumptions and to invite honest self-examination.

- **Step 3 – Options:** The coach elicits suggestions from the client by asking effective questions and guides him/her towards decisions.

- **Step 4 – Way Forward:** Coach and client commit to action, define a timeframe for their objectives and identify how to overcome obstacles.

Get Out of Your Own Way

*"As long as a man stands in his own way,
everything seems to be in his way."*

RALPH WALDO EMERSON, PHILOSOPHER & POET

Gremlins pop up sometimes and we need to tame them. Gremlins sabotage our best-laid plans and often they tell us that we shouldn't try anything different in case we fail or make a fool of ourselves. When no-one is looking have a go at saying stop!

Our core beliefs that run our lives often sound like this: 'I can't do that – I'm not good enough'. In order to gain freedom from these drivers we need to take full responsibility for all the events that have happened to us. Give up the 'why me' story and transform it into 'this is my journey and I needed to learn some key lessons from this'. This is the place of power from which you can alter your reality. Create an internal dialogue that empowers you.

Journaling is a good tool to identify any gremlins. The focus is on forgiveness and expressing what is holding you back without judgment. Also, we can use our body to lead our brain. As soon as a negative comment comes into your mind, change your body posture to the way you would stand if you were feeling strong and confident. You can also imagine the negative thought as a comically ridiculous voice or cartoon character. That will distance you from their impact.

Do you want it bad enough to face your fears? Start by changing your internal statements to questions, for example: 'I am bored stiff of my job' to: 'Could I be excited by my job?' 'I make no difference to the organisation' becomes 'Could I make a difference to the organisation?' Our need to play small or stay safe prevents us from committing fully to our lives. Would you prefer to stay in a job you hate or risk creating a business you absolutely love? Would you rather be right about feeling powerless or be wrong about your ability to surpass your wildest expectations of yourself?

If you knew you had six months to live would you continue what you are doing now?

Say to yourself: 'I am worthy of having what I desire and I am going to do whatever it takes to fulfil my aspirations.' Let the universe guide you towards this now. When you become focused about your direction, the universe collaborates to meet your needs in what may seem to be mere coincidences. The eminent psychologist, Carl Jung, termed this as 'Synchronicity'. If you are mindful of these circumstances you will progress in leaps and bounds. I encourage my clients to open their eyes to this remarkable phenomenon.

Keeping your word is so important for change. Even if it is a small task like making a list of things to do everyday, if you don't do it you are telling the universe and yourself that you cannot be counted on. Breaking our promises wears down our self-respect. Treat your word like gold and it will deliver gold. If you are not going to do it, don't say it.

Is it worth it to invest your time and energy to achieve your dreams? This is your decision to make – there is no magic carpet ride to wherever you want to be in your life. Everything you need to change already lies within you. Take small significant steps and you will see the payoff. Analyse your excuses. Do they hinder your progress to achieving your dreams?

Do you feel anxious when someone tells you to go with the flow, maybe lighten up a bit? Do you like to hold on with a tight grip to feel in control? Often the last thing we can imagine doing is becoming passive as there is a strong belief in our culture that you have to achieve and be doing things to be powerful. Passive energy has its own kind of strength. Surrender is not weakness or loss. It is powerful non-resistance which gives birth to our higher self.

Whenever I go past a cemetery I look at the stones representing those that were once living with cares, worries, ambitions, losses and bad hair days and ask myself: 'Where are they now?' It reminds me to ask myself: 'What's important to me in this moment? What is vital to me now?' It doesn't matter if you are stuck as long as you are happy to be alive. Only people who have suffered enough emotionally realise that it is the self that perpetuates all emotional suffering. Get out of your own way.

If you are a boss you will want your workers to do their best work for you and not burn effigies of you behind your back! Recognise workers as human beings, not as machines. Lao Tsu advised leaders to demonstrate humanity, compassion and mercy as signs of strength. We've been trained to be tough and go-getting and to look upon gentleness as the soft side where you are vulnerable. The Tao on the other hand teaches that the true sign of strength is that you can afford to be gentle. The golden rule – respect, both yourself and others.

If you find your staff are not being creative or acting autonomously maybe you need to consider whether they are always being told what to do. Instead try giving directional guidance and coaching them so that they have the space to grow, express themselves and deliver their ideas on time.

OBSTACLE 1:
"I'M SO STRESSED, BUT IF I RELAX I'LL LOSE MY EDGE AND FAIL."

Are you so busy that you never have time to slow down, breathe deeply and enjoy life? Are you in fact afraid to slow down because you've told yourself that you can't afford to? Or perhaps you have convinced yourself that you thrive on the adrenalin? If this is you, then I'm willing to bet that your stress is an avoidance tactic; a distraction to keep your mind busy so that it does not focus on the things you'd rather remain in denial about.

In this way, workaholism can become a form of escape. But remember: no one ever escaped their way to fulfilment, so it is important to become conscious again. Just recognising this pattern at work is a big step in the right direction. Consider if you are the sort of person who only feels okay when they are running around in some kind of conflict. Stop and take time to really see what is going on in your life. Allow your instinct to tell you what needs to be done – this requires some quiet reflection time.

CASE STUDY

Jill was a company director in her early forties. She ran a small financial consultancy which provided specialist training to staff in investment banks. She was not making as much money as she wanted, yet she was rushed off her feet and could not see how she could try any harder than she already was. Her life and business were both in chaos and she was lurching from one crisis to the next. The problem Jill was having is one I often see in people who have started businesses. Jill was very gifted at what she *did* – understanding complex financial concepts and teaching them to others – but she was not gifted at *managing*. In fact, she did not have a clue how to manage her staff, her time *or* her finances.

The crunch had come when she was about to start a two-day training course at a leading bank and she was still in the office at 9.00 pm the night before with her slide presentation unfinished, yelling at her assistant.

When she first came to see me Jill was convinced her problem stemmed from the fact there simply were not enough hours in the day. So I got Jill to keep a diary for the next two weeks, noting exactly how she spent her time. It was enlightening to say the least.

At our next session I helped Jill to divide all her activities into four categories. The most effective time management models I've seen use variations of these same distinctions:

1. Urgent and important - must be done and must be done now.
2. Urgent but not important - those things that interrupt us and take us away from our true objectives.

---

3. Important but not urgent - the more time a person spends on activities in this category, the more fulfilled they will be. It can involve work or non-work activities; ideally there should be a mix of the two.

4. Not important and not urgent - mindless activities like watching rubbish on TV. US motivational speaker Tony Robbins calls this 'the zone of escape'.

Categories one and three include all the important activities. This is where successful, fulfilled people spend most of their time. Remember: 'important' does not necessarily mean 'work-related', although items in category one usually are. It could mean taking a scuba-diving course in Mauritius if that is what fires you up, or learning to salsa dance. You are in the zone of fulfilment whenever you are following your passions and growing as a person.

Categories two and four are the thieves of fulfilment. However, the majority of people squander away their lives in these zones. And I was unsurprised to learn, on looking at Jill's diary, that this was where she had been spending almost all of her time. An example of 'urgent but not important', the zone in which Jill spent most of her time, is having your computer set up to interrupt you with a 'ding' every time an e-mail comes in. And stopping whatever you are doing to answer every e-mail. This was one of the habits Jill admitted to.

She also allowed herself to get held up on long and unproductive phone-calls, even at times when she was already late meeting a client deadline. Jill was an action illusionist: because she was always busy she assumed she must be achieving things. Yet the most important things in her life and business were not being done, simply because she never gave herself time to do them.

After that session I got Jill to carry on with her diary, but this time with a constant consciousness of whether what she was doing was leading her towards fulfilment or away from it. This new-found awareness led to a gradual shift away from the time-wasting activities and towards productive ones. Jill had freed up a great deal of time, and it had knock-on effects throughout her life and business. For example, because she now felt less rushed she not only treated her employees better; she was also able to set aside time to learn about managing people.

REFLECT

Do you thrive on being busy but feel anxious any time it is just you alone with your thoughts? The more uncomfortable you feel sitting in silence with your thoughts, the more important it is that you slow down. When you are centred you become part of the solution.

OBSTACLE 2:
"I'M AFRAID TO LEAVE MY COMFORT ZONE!"

Do you lack confidence? Are you afraid of being different; of taking a stand and being noticed? Do you have difficulty expressing yourself at work? Are you so afraid of making a mistake that your creativity is smothered, and you are valuing what people think of you over what you know you are contributing?

The comfort zone is all about certainty: it is an attachment to what is familiar, secure and comfortable coupled with a fear of the unknown. We all need some certainty in our lives. However, I firmly believe that the less certainty you can live with, the greater your quality of life will be. Sadly, most people need a great deal of certainty. In their pursuit of this they miss out on all manner of exciting opportunities and new experiences.

Can you imagine what it would be like to be fearless? To embrace new challenges, situations and people with joyful enthusiasm and curiosity instead of with miserable fear and suspicion?

CASE STUDY

Raj, an I.T analyst came to me with a common problem. He was desperate to break out of his rut and take on challenges, but was paralysed with fear. For example, his head was buzzing with ideas, yet in every staff meeting he sat silent, afraid to open his mouth for fear of sounding stupid. In fact, his only goal during meetings was to avoid getting called on to speak, so he spent them avoiding eye contact with anyone. All this was having a limiting effect on the projects he was given to work on. He also suspected

---

it was one of the reasons he kept getting passed over for promotion. That and his underlying belief that he was not as 'clever' as his highly qualified colleagues.

The first thing we looked at was why he felt that what he had to contribute would be stupid or unwelcome. It was the first time he had ever questioned this. What was he gaining by not sharing his views? What was certain was that he was losing a lot more than he was gaining. He soon realised that what he called his comfort zone was in fact not comfortable at all. He was tired of playing small and wasting his potential.

I got him to visualise himself speaking up and his colleagues and superiors being impressed with his ideas – ideas which turned out to be extremely valuable to the company. I also got him to identify a role model; the person he would most like to emulate in this area. When breaking through old habits and building better ones it can be very helpful to have someone to model. He chose Richard Branson for his bold, innovative brilliance. He imagined how Branson would act sitting at the boardroom table: what would his body language be like, how would he voice his ideas? He also imagined Branson cheering him on and patting him on the back after he delivered his ideas!

The first time Raj spoke up it was easier than he thought it would be and he was delighted with the response he got. He was suddenly on the radar of his superiors and as a result he was given the responsibility he knew he could handle. When Raj and I parted ways, it was with him feeling confident that next time there was an opening for someone at his level of the company to be moved to the next, he stood a great chance. He also realised that courage is often better rewarded than qualifications and a high I.Q.

REFLECT

*"Comfort starts as a servant
and becomes a master."*

KAHLIL GIBRAN, AUTHOR OF 'THE PROPHET'

Comfort zones slowly paralyse us, but we get so used to hanging out there that we don't feel the stiffness until much later. Hindu and Buddhist philosophy maintain that permanence and security are illusions. Apathy is the same – a belief in our powerlessness that keeps us stuck. It manifests as learned helplessness – the belief that all of one's past experience are evidence of the utter futility of trying to change one's life. When we throw an endless string of excuses on every opportunity, we exhaust ourselves and everyone around us. Even those who want to support us burn out and may even start to avoid us.

We all know how quickly pleasure can turn into pain. It's easy to get attached even to negative things – the devil you know. Change is the only constant. If you think that the best times are behind you then they probably are. As Anais Nin observed: *"We don't see things as they are, we see things as we are"*. Focus on your future – you have your whole life ahead of you. Expect good things to happen. When things turn out in your favour see it as a part of a wider pattern of events. This will help you in times of difficulty. How often do you try new things? Think of new ways you can open up your world to new possibilities.

OBSTACLE 3:
"I'M DRIVEN BY WINNING AT ALL COSTS."

Do you focus mainly on your reputation? Is being known, being highly successful and having powerful influence very important to you? Are you good at psychological warfare, taking unfair advantage of others' weakness? Do you want to win at all costs and you have no qualms about manipulating things to appear powerful? One-upmanship and power control can be addictive emotions. The results are always short-lived.

CASE STUDY

Andrew was a lawyer in his fifties. Although he was highly competent in court and in front of clients, he was a disaster at managing his staff. His sharp intellect may have been an asset in the courtroom, but in the office he used it as a weapon. He had gained a reputation as a bully, though he did not know this until he was faced with some feedback from staff. When his superiors presented him with his first 360-degree appraisal – something his firm had recently introduced – he was stunned. His subordinates were almost without exception very unhappy with the way he was managing them. And one member of staff had even written that she was ashamed to work for him.

When Andrew reflected on his behaviour at work, he realised the comments were justified. But this was the first time he had ever considered how his work persona might affect others. When he came to see me, it was to find out how he could change for the better. He had no idea where to start. First we needed to look at how he'd got into these negative patterns in the first place. He had no real joy in his life, he confided. It was as if he was under a cloud of

---

anxiety all the time. He took this out on others. He also had a guiding belief that he had to be on the offensive at all times; if he let his guard down and took a softly-softly approach he would lose his edge.

I got him to examine these statements one by one – to hold each up to the light of inquiry – and see how true they were. Gradually, Andrew realised that the very defence mechanisms he thought were protecting him were actually sabotaging him. He would be much more effective at work if he was able to interact with his staff in a way which got them on his side and got the best out of them. Similarly, if he made relaxation a priority so that he wasn't always on a knife-edge of stress, he would do his own work more effectively.

The 360-degree appraisal was Andrew's initial catalyst for change and he used it as a powerful motivating factor. He was determined that the next appraisal – six months after the first – would be a very different matter altogether.

REFLECT

See how you do at this quiz:

1. Name the five wealthiest people in the world.
2. Name the last five winners of the Miss World contest.
3. Name five people who have won the Nobel or Pulitzer Prize.
4. Name the last five Academy Award winners for best actor and actress.

How did you do?

Here's another quiz. See how you do on this one:

1. List a few teachers who aided your journey through school.

2. Name three friends who have helped you through a difficult time.
3. Name five people who have taught you something worthwhile.
4. Think of a few people who have made you feel appreciated and special.

The moral is we remember what is personal and important to us and besides over time applause and achievements fade away. Don't be surprised if you feel like writing a few thank you notes after the second quiz!

The Emerging Force Within

*"This is the true joy in life, the being used
for a purpose recognized by yourself as a
mighty one; the being thoroughly worn out
before you are thrown on the scrap heap;
the being a force of nature instead of a feverish
selfish little clod of ailments and grievances
complaining that the world will not devote
itself to making you happy."*

GEORGE BERNARD SHAW, IRISH PLAYWRIGHT

If you feel your work or life are lacking in meaning and purpose you are not alone. In fact, so many people have this experience that it has come to seem almost normal. Yet few are truly happy living this way. Our time here is precious – literally irreplaceable.

Many of my clients find it helpful during our sessions to talk and reflect about their purpose and the meaning they attach to their work. Most realise that current uncertainty about their purpose is not the same as having a purposeless life. Consider a man who, looking back on his life after 66 years, thought he was a failure: Winston Churchill. He was a soldier, journalist, parliamentarian and author before he was 25. He held a wide variety of powerful positions in government but felt worthless because he had failed to attain the office of prime minister.

His time came, of course. Hindsight being 20/20 we can see that his earlier experiences were a necessary preparation for the highest office and that he would not have been the great leader he was if this responsibility had been granted to him before he was ready for it. You don't jump from nowhere to somewhere. You are always somewhere. Even if you don't want to be where you are now it is still a point on your path. You may feel you have missed your calling, but you may not realise you are exactly where you are supposed to be at this point in time. You just don't see the links yet. You may be engaged in something crucially important for you without realising it.

All of us move towards our calling in stages, taking with us all the resources we have accumulated over the years. There is no substitute for constant inner exploration. We do not always discover ourselves in a blinding flash of insight. But we can start right here, right now.

Madeleine Albright preceded her monumental political career with being a mother, charity fundraiser and getting a PhD. She brought with her a range of well-honed, transferable skills. These skills we sometimes dismiss when looking at what options we have to find fulfilling work. Developing passion is a process of transition – it is not about making rash knee-jerk decisions where we expect instant approval for our plans to be the next Lakshmi Mittal, the steel billionaire. Doing what you love doesn't have to involve years of training – it can even happen out of apparent disaster.

Are you bored? This is a common consequence of lack of purpose. No one is bored in a crisis. In a disaster, everyone has a purpose: self-preservation. The psychologist Abraham

Maslow's[3] hierarchy of needs describes five different levels of human need, each building on the last. At the bottom are the 'physiological' needs; if we do not have food, water, air and shelter all our efforts go to securing these until we do.

At the next level are the 'safety' needs: finding stability and consistency in a chaotic world. Levels three and four are our needs for love and esteem, and it is only with the foundation of these four that we can reach the fifth level: self-actualisation, which Maslow described as: *"Becoming more and more what one is. Becoming everything one is capable of being"*. It is at this level that attention turns to the search for knowledge, peace, self-fulfilment, oneness with God and so on.

While in one sense having everything you need and want in the material world is a luxury enjoyed by only a fraction of people, it is a double-edged sword. The feeling of having no more mountains to climb can be debilitating. Alexander The Great supposedly wept because he had no more worlds to conquer.

I'm not recommending you create crisis to keep yourself stimulated! Do you really need regular brushes with death in order to feel alive? No. Spiritual work presents you with internal mountains to climb. However, sometimes we need to rip back to the wild to refresh ourselves. Whatever reconnects you to the natural world is the surest way to regain perspective. It rekindles an appreciation of life itself. Understanding that life is a great gift and enjoying all the things you do – these are great antidotes to purposelessness.

---

[3] Abraham Maslow first introduced the concept of his hierarchy of needs in his 1943 paper 'A Theory Of Human Motivation' published in *Psychological Review*, Issue 50.

However, the best way of all to counteract feelings of emptiness is to help someone else. At work, this could mean taking a real interest in and supporting your trainees.

In his book, *The Power of Now*, Eckhart Tolle talks about the concept of 'waiting': *"Give up waiting as a state of mind. When you catch yourself slipping into waiting, snap out of it. Come into the present moment. Just be, and enjoy being. If you are present, there is never any need for you to wait for anything."*

There is also this craze to be famous that is very popular today especially in young people. We're convinced that we were born with a special mission or calling that someday we and others will recognise. We remain waiting for this and stuck in the interval stage. Yet if we don't let go of the need to be special, we can't create our calling because we will continue to look outside of ourselves for a 'call' that only comes from within.

OBSTACLE 1:
"MY JOB DOES NOT INSPIRE ME ENOUGH."

Do you feel that you have missed your true vocation in life? Are you just showing up at the office each day to pay the mortgage, with no real passion for your work? Does the clock move slowest of all during working hours? Are your work goals personally fulfilling, or are they just to please your boss or earn you a commission? Remember you are also competing against people who love their work and if you are only working for the money you are likely to be blown away by the competition. Dedication shines every time.

CASE STUDY

Gianni was an accountant in his mid-thirties. He was quite happy at work, but what he really wanted to be, he told me, was a chef. He loved experimenting with food and creating new dishes, and friends and family had told him that he had real talent. He was an avid reader of cookery books and would travel miles on expeditions to find rare ingredients. As this passion increased he felt more and more certain that he should give up his job and open a restaurant. He needed no training, he assured me at our first session; he already knew how to cook! He envisaged himself in charge and at the creative helm, just like he was in his kitchen at home. He even started to swear like Gordon Ramsay!

So I got him to do some detailed research into what he would have to do to make his dream a reality. What he discovered shocked him. Gianni had had a romantic notion that he could borrow a modest amount of money to open a restaurant on a shoe-string and then expand into somewhere bigger and better. However, his research showed him just how competitive the restaurant business is and what a financial risk he would be taking. As the bank would use his house as collateral against any loan, he decided that it was too risky to take this route to becoming a chef, especially as he had a wife and two young children.

This left him with the option of undertaking formal chef's training and then working his way up the ranks in restaurant and hotel kitchens, starting, of course, in the lowliest positions. The thought of spending weeks peeling potatoes did not appeal; nor was this option much better from a financial perspective. While he was training he would use up most of his savings as he'd still have to support his family, and initially he would earn a fraction of what he now earned as an accountant. And in the harsh, competitive world of the restaurant kitchen there was no guarantee he would ever reach his current salary. In addition, not only would he have to work longer hours; they were also considerably less sociable hours, as anyone who is serious about success in the restaurant business must kiss goodbye to evenings, weekends and holidays.

This exercise helped Gianni get clarity that although cooking was his passion, it did not need to be his career. Once Gianni was clear about this, he was free to begin fully indulging his passion right away. He decided how much time he'd like to be able to spend on it every week and scheduled this in his diary, making it a priority. And he made his next holiday a cookery course in Italy!

Coaching guided Gianni to the realisation that he could live his passion outside of his career, but for many it has the opposite outcome: it is the catalyst that finally gives them the courage to take the brave step they have needed to take for a long time.

Doing what you love will often offer you greater prosperity in the long term, but sometimes it won't. Sometimes when you do what you really enjoy, you *need* less money.

REFLECT

Finding meaning is an ongoing challenge. Think about the inevitable passage of time and your best use of it. Unguarded time slips away. Find meaning in the small moments of ordinary life, rather than just wasting them. Use anything that comes your way for your personal evolution. Living this way allows us to be more than we would otherwise have been. It is about being fully present in every moment, even if you are just filing some papers. For evolution requires an engagement with, not a withdrawal from, life itself. Don't go through the motions – enjoy every meal by tasting each mouthful; talk to a colleague and hear every word. Pay attention to the moments in your life and refuse to live it in a hurry. Affirm to yourself: *I have plenty of time. How long it takes is how long it takes.*

OBSTACLE 2:
"I DON'T KNOW WHAT I WANT!"

Are you unfulfilled but confused about what it would take to change that? Do you lack a clear picture of what fulfilment would look and feel like for you? Work is a journey for most people. Not everyone leaves school with a clear idea of what their calling is; far from it. But finding your vocation in life is one of the surest ways to fulfilment. You may need to dig a bit for your talents and try many things. How will you know unless you do?

These days most people hold a variety of jobs in different fields during the course of their lives. Some things we need to learn from experience, and that means that sometimes you have to do a job to discover you are not suited to it. You haven't wasted your time as long as you make use of what you've learned when making your next decision.

No matter how long your father has treasured his vision of you making it as a cabinet minister, if rummaging for antiques in car boot sales is more your thing, go ahead and take a part-time job with an auctioneer and a day job to pay the mortgage. You will be living authentically. Besides you are not here to fulfil the dreams of frustrated parents!

Unless you grant yourself the flexibility to pursue different purposes during your life, you could end up like the most popular kid in school still reliving your past glory years twenty years later without a new vision. We are not made to do just one thing. Don't cling to any one thing, stretching it beyond its time. Like overblown bubble gum it may pop. If you have succeeded in the past, no one can take your memories away from you. But they won't last forever. Nothing does.

You can re-live those memories, but you need to let go sometime. You might not find another purpose until you can do this. It isn't easy, which is why we can all relate to the image of the popular kid who can't move on. It's a condition which finds its way into my consulting room regularly. It takes courage to move on. There is some good news here: Carl Jung, believed the greatest potential for growth is in the second half of life. He noticed that to carry on with the same goals we had when we were younger can make us feel rejected and failures. Finding a way to stop looking backwards and to look to who and what we can become is an important step.

Whenever I feel a sense of despondency and miss the cut and thrust of my youth, my father's wise words give me a source of strength that calms me to a more accepting state. He reminds me that the brightest future will always be based on a forgotten past and that I can't move forward in life until I let go of my past disappointments and heartaches. We all need to spend quiet time assimilating our life's experiences and by doing so we come to accept ourselves. By getting to know my beliefs and putting behind me memories of less-than-perfect behaviour I have found new ways to be comfortable in my own new skin. Shedding the old has led to many unexpected gifts and adventures in my life that I am so grateful for.

CASE STUDY

Rania came to see me because she was going back to work after a 20-year career break during which she had raised three children. Her problem was that she didn't know what she wanted to do. She had been a secretary until the age of 26 when she got married and had her first child. Now she wanted to try something different. But as a woman in her late forties, with little work experience and no qualifications, what were her options? She was terrified that she may become invisible and drop out of view like her mother had in her forties. She still dreamed of making her mark, but felt a little overwhelmed by entering uncharted territory.

So our first task was to brainstorm all the things she enjoyed and was good at. At first we didn't seem to be getting anywhere as Rania initially drew a complete blank. Rania had the look of someone jaded by the disappointments in her life. I encouraged her to start a journal of her dreams. If money was no object and she could not fail, what would she like to do? If she woke up one morning and overnight her fairy godmother had granted her wish, what is the first thing she would notice? This is when her floodgates finally opened. She could think of lots of things that fit these criteria but still nothing really stood out. However, as she reflected further a clear pattern began to emerge. Rania was really interested in anything to do with gardens, plants and flowers.

She had long pursued this as a hobby and had occasionally thought of turning it into a career, but the idea had always been quickly chased out of her mind by self-defeating thoughts. In fact, these same thoughts followed hot on the heels of her bringing up this idea during our session. I got her to look at them logically and see whether they were really true. Was it really true, for example that she was too old to start this new venture, or that she could never make money out of it? Of course not! There were plenty of role models around to contradict this negative thought and in any case I asked Rania to consider the *advantages* of age and she came up with a handful. Her emotional state changed from fear to curiosity and a little excitement!

Rania needed hardcore evidence that age was no barrier to starting a new business, so I gave this to her. More than 60% of new successful businesses are in the hands of the over fifties in the U.K. She also realised that her well-honed feminine talents of intuition and interpersonal skills are crucial in business.

A few months after she identified her chosen career Rania had researched the market and what it would take to be successful in it. First of all she'd need professional training. She found a full-time course that would give her the education and expertise needed to turn her passion into a career. I taught Rania to relax during this time when she was naturally a little anxious. She learned some deep breathing methods which helped her to face her fears and to muster up patience. We discussed any obstacles she might face that could slow her down. She made peace with these without fighting them or wishing they would go away. Thinking 'if only' adds power to the obstacles and takes power away from you.

I taught Rania a visualisation technique to help her entrench her passion where she imagined seeing herself on a movie screen going through the experience of success and accomplishing all she wanted flawlessly. The idea is to see this image large, bright and colourful, adding sound, feelings, smells and tastes. I taught her to activate as many of her five senses as possible. For example she could see herself designing award-winning landscape plans on large paper, smelling the roses and freesias which she adored and touching the fresh soil with her rubber gloves. Rania could even hear the accolades she receives from delighted clients and the media! Too right – you must always step up and enjoy the rewards.

There was gratitude written all over her face as she smiled. I saw Rania's body posture literally transform in minutes as these powerful changes began to take root right down to the cellular level. She stood tall as she appreciated the results of her efforts. She had come a long way in her mind and it was only a matter of time before this would become her new reality. She saw the new, confident her on the movie screen in her mind and I asked her to integrate this new image by stepping into it and becoming one with this new her.

Rania embraced this technique with a tremendous amount of joy and because she gave herself the permission to overcome her hang-ups, she started to believe that she was very capable of starting her own business. Feeling unstoppable she had tears in her eyes as she thought she had lost this determination over the years. I used an NLP technique called 'Anchoring' which Rania repeated everyday and she reported that she felt a power and strength growing inside as she kept adding more real-life details to the imagery.

When something you see, hear or feel, taste or smell consistently changes your state or you consistently respond in the same way, this is an example of anchoring. An example of a visual anchor is a smile; music can be an auditory anchor.

They build habits. Rania felt an emotional freedom from being aware of the anchors she had and choosing to respond to the ones she wanted. She kept this resourceful state and after her training she immediately started a landscape gardening business and is also enjoying running weekend courses teaching children about horticulture.

How does it feel to stand in the shoes of an optimist? Try out a new way of seeing the world, a new way of speaking and hearing. What are the possibilities you can create when you ask questions like 'what if' that open doors, rather than the 'why me' which slams the door shut in your face?

REFLECT

Herman Hesse won the Nobel Prize in Literature, but earlier in life he seriously considered suicide. His talent as a writer blossomed later, but in the meantime he couldn't see the purpose in his life. However, the difficulties he had faced in his own life, illuminated in his writing, inspired a generation to consider enlightenment and inner meaning. Yet this purpose was lost on him as he struggled in his earlier years. He toughed it out until things got better. If you exercise patience and courage – two cardinal virtues – change will come.

OBSTACLE 3:
"I'M DRIVEN BY FINANCIAL WORRIES."

Do you find that there is never quite enough money to enable you to live the life you want? Or maybe you *do* have the financial resources to live the life you want, but mortgage, holiday home, car payments and school fees are all conspiring to keep you trapped in a job you dislike.

How many of the things you purchase every day do you really need? Have you ever wondered about that? We have departed so far from our real necessities, that many of us are not even capable of determining the difference between luxury and vital needs. Ask yourself: do I need all this to be happy?

What you regard as normal today could become luxury for you tomorrow... or the other way around: obsolete. It all depends on how life treats you... or how *you* treat life. The worst thing you can do is to take things for granted: a high-flying job, a six-figure salary, a great spouse, a nice house, or even something as simple as a mobile phone!

CASE STUDY

Richard was the global head of communications at a blue-chip company. In his early forties, he was happily married with four children. "Although, I must admit, not as happily married as I used to be," he confided. Richard hardly ever saw his wife or children as he was working such long hours. And when he was home he was so burnt out that all we wanted to do was sleep or read the papers.

He worked, on average, 60 hours a week and spent an additional hour a day commuting. He also travelled a lot, sometimes two weeks out of a month. It did not leave much time for his marriage, nor did he have much of a relationship

---

with his children. He was deeply unhappy with this and so was the rest of the family. When Richard first came to see me it was for advice on how to relax and how to increase his energy levels. Although he hated his job, changing to a less demanding one wasn't an option for him, he told me. He couldn't afford to. Yet when I quizzed him about this it became clear he did not really have a clue where his money was going. So the first thing I got him to do was to take a really close look at his outgoings.

I explained that I did not need to know his financial business; I just wanted him to review his expenditure and see whether he was right. His four children were in private school and that cost over £40,000 a year. But that was an essential expense, he told me. Fair enough. As we looked over the rest it was a different story. He and his family lived in a bigger house than they needed, in one of the more expensive areas of London. They also had a luxury holiday home in France that they rarely visited more than twice a year. Gourmet restaurants, ski trips, astronomical mobile phone bills (especially with four kids), he was, quite simply, haemorrhaging cash.

All of this is fine if you can afford it − afford it meaning, if what you have to do to maintain that lifestyle is leaving you fulfilled, joyful and at peace. Nothing could be further from the truth for Richard. But he was starting to realise he had choices he never knew existed. He went through the family finances with his wife and they realised that he could afford to halve his salary and they would still live very comfortably. It took a while for this to sink in, but what it meant was that the weight hanging round his shoulders for so long was lifted. After much reflection, Richard ended up taking a more fulfilling job in a smaller company. Not only did he enjoy his hours at work more; he also had a lot more time to devote to other things in his life.

REFLECT

"Many men go fishing all of their lives without knowing that it is not the fish they're after."

HENRY DAVID THOREAU, AMERICAN PHILOSOPHER

Decide from the outset that you are going to be true to your core values. Pursue your life's purpose with the intention of being the very best you can be, rather than focusing primarily upon financial rewards. You can certainly have a monetary goal. However, just be aware of the danger of letting this become the primary motive. Continually re-assess the balance between your externally-focused activities and your spiritual goals. Never let that balance slip. When we find our true calling and trust that what we put forth from our inner self will be of value to others, we will receive what we need to live in exchange.

Harmony At Work

"It is amazing what can be accomplished when nobody cares about who gets the credit."

ROBERT YATES, UNITED STATES POLITICIAN

In any organisation, toxic emotions – negative emotions that 'infect' an environment – can have a significant impact on that organisation's ability to motivate or retain staff. Computer viruses are not the only viruses that spread and cause havoc in the operations of business. We pay far more attention to computer virus attacks and spend a fortune in virus protection programmes but we disregard the other debilitating infections in the workplace.

We live in a world where judgments are made quickly and lies are told by an irresponsible press. People tear down others' reputations like it's a national sport. At work we must learn not to take things personally. All great leaders faced attack and opposition – Jesus, Gandhi, Martin Luther King, to name just a few. It is the *fear* of attack which is the greatest cause of millions of us leading mediocre lives. We would rather do nothing than face being true to ourselves and take on the responsibility of being a leader. It takes courage to stand out and speak up when others are silent. Facing an attack often helps you discover an untapped inner strength. In the midst of criticism ask yourself this: am I acting with integrity and responding with truth in my heart to what is being said? If your answer is yes, stick to it and abandon the rest.

Courage to ride through criticism is a very useful quality to have. Oprah Winfrey[4] once said: *"Every single bit of pain I have experienced in my life was a result of me worrying about what another person was thinking of me"*. How much time and energy do you waste trying to get external validation? How different would your life be if you could let go of that need?

Make peace with the reality that it is impossible to please everyone. Here is your new motto: "What other people think of me is none of my business." Repeat this statement to yourself often. Are you trying to control things that are *outside* of your control? Like how other people react, or what they think of you? Resolve today that you will let go of all stress about things you cannot control. Focus your energy on the things you can influence.

The martial art Aikido teaches us about being strong without ever harming someone who is in conflict with us. It has been defined as a 'way of blending energy'.

I wonder what it would be like to experiment with forgiveness at work? How would you begin? Well, maybe simply by reflecting on those workplace situations that annoy or grieve you, or in which you have been mistreated or wronged. We create rules in our head for how people should behave. Resenting people for ignoring our rules is crazy. We can't punish anyone by refusing to forgive them.

Try letting yourself feel the feelings associated with those experiences - without acting on them. Sometimes wisdom

---

[4] Laura B Randolph. Oprah opens up about her weight, her wedding and why she withheld the book – Oprah Winfrey – Cover Story. Ebony Magazine, October 1993.

emerges from such reflecting and a way towards forgiveness and useful action emerges just by your making room for the feelings and waiting quietly beside them. Often any attack on you is about them and not you. Realise that people come from the limit of their own growth and experience – do not allow them to press your 'hot buttons'. Keep moving forward in your mind to the next positive episode in your life.

Break it down into easy steps. The first step is to stop saying or doing unkind things even if you feel you have been wronged. The truth is you are probably nursing your hurt: rehearsing it in your imagination, talking to others about it, plotting fantasy revenge... you know the routine. You can't change the actions of that person, but you can change your own.

Step two is to let go of the anger and try to forgive. Some people find strength by praying for the other person. Others hold onto the issue and keep it alive and suffer. If you can move forward without recriminations, things will change – there will be a shift in attitude somewhere along the line – and sooner than you think.

It reminds me of the wry wisdom in my mother's words: "Failing to forgive another person is like taking poison and expecting that other person to die." Take a look at the poisons you take at work – and, maybe, even choose to stop taking them! Then breathe a deep sigh of relief! You are free. When you let go of things, they let go of you.

OBSTACLE 1:
"I HAVE TOXIC COLLEAGUES!"

Any time people come together there will be personal differences. You don't usually choose the people you work with, so extra effort is often required to keep the office harmonious. When people are faced with a hostile work environment they tend to forget the things they did to start or keep the ball rolling. Take home message: What we think, say and do has consequences. Too often we act as if we were unfamiliar with that kind of responsibility in the workplace.

You can't completely dissolve all friction in the office, but you can dissolve your stress at being caught up in the tension. As with everything in life it is not the situations you are faced with so much as your *reaction* to them that will determine your experience. Instead of getting drawn into the situation and getting angry, take a deep breath and see the affirmative qualities about this person or situation. What are their good qualities? As you find the upside of that which makes you feel bad, imagine what other gifts are hidden. What difficult and unnerving possibilities or lessons are you avoiding? It diffuses the situation immediately and puts things into perspective.

When we learn respect for our peers we can come to accept their differences. We can learn to use those differences for our mutual benefit. Along with respect comes acceptance of the inherent right of each person to follow their chosen life path, and also that diversity and variety lead to a rich mixture of humanity. Without respect we have only conflict and hostility.

Think of it as a partnership. Encourage a balanced and fair way of being and working together. Use honest disagreement rather than hostility as a way forward. The attempt by us to achieve total self-sufficiency and independence emerges from the illusory separateness of the ego. As we participate in economic life we learn that we are part of an interdependent web of complex interactions and changes in one part of the web affect all of us involved. Establishing just, harmonious and honest relationships is the key to economic well-being for all.

CASE STUDY

Benjamin worked for the brokerage arm of a large investment bank. When he came to see me he'd been there three months. His problem was that he could not stand his colleagues! Gossip was the currency in this office; it was what people exchanged as a token of friendship. But it was far from friendly to whoever's back happened to be turned at the time. Benjamin knew that he, too, was getting this treatment once out of earshot and it made him uneasy.

More worrying to him, he had, out of desire for approval, allowed himself to be pulled into this cruel sport and become one of the office's most vicious satirists. He was now anxious to stop. Problem was he had fallen into a pattern of talking in this way with certain colleagues. How would he break that pattern?

The first thing we established is that the only person he had control over was himself. However, he needed to realise that the control he had was complete and existed for a reason. I asked him what sort of person he wanted to be in the office. He told me he wanted to be someone who acted with integrity. He decided that from now on every word he uttered about another person would be in line with how he'd like others to speak about him. And I reminded him that if he treated others this way, it wouldn't be long before that was the very treatment he himself was getting back.

So we prepared what he would say and how he would act next time one of his colleagues approached him at the water fountain fishing for gossip. He had various ways of handling this, depending on how the conversation panned out. He would start by simply sticking to saying only positive things; in many instances this would be sufficient. However, if he was pushed he could make his position clear; state firmly that he had decided not to speak negatively anymore.

Benjamin did just this and the results were astonishing to him. He found that when he did not feed the gossip others put in front of him, it soon died. Also, by raising his own standards he had created a new way of interacting for others to flow into. On the whole, the colleagues to whom Benjamin explained his change in behaviour reacted by saying how pleased they were, as they had been unhappy with the negative mood in the office too. Not everyone felt the same, of course. Those who could not give up the gossip habit carried on as before. But over time they were in a minority.

REFLECT

In Judaism there is a sin know as *loshon hara*, which refers to engaging in gossip. Speaking negatively about someone for no constructive purpose is equivalent to cursing them, and listening in on gossip is as bad as spreading it yourself because you are actively participating in it.

Do you get tempted to join in the office politics?

OBSTACLE 2:
"MY BOSS MAKES MY LIFE HELL!"

One of the complaints I hear most often is about difficult bosses. This problem goes all the way back to caveman times, I'm sure! Of course, one option is finding a new job, but there is no guarantee the new boss will be any better. The people in our life are our teachers. It doesn't mean you have to like them. If your boss makes you angry, then this is your opportunity to learn to deal with your anger effectively. You have a practice buddy! Continually ask yourself: 'What am I learning from this?'

Every experience we go through is a mirror. If we are unhappy the experience provides us with an opportunity to change our thoughts, create new energies and respond differently. Start looking closely at what goes on between your ears. Change that and you can change your life. It's a choice you make. This determines our place in the world.

People who have problems with their bosses, especially if this problem tends to follow them from job to job, often have unresolved issues around authority. It indicates an emotional charge attached to authority, and may also point to unresolved business with parents which may need attention.

Just because your boss criticises you it doesn't mean he is right and you should start to panic about your job security. Your boss needs you too. Don't take it personally; it's just the pecking order. Don't get into the vicious circle of taking it out on those over whom you have authority. Do your work to the best of your abilities and take the high road of refusing to get caught up in it.

Make him look good in front of others. Actively listen to his concerns. He will find greater trust in you and this will be the start of a mutually comfortable relationship in the office. Notice how the energy around you both becomes lighter and free-flowing. He will be more willing to accept your ideas.

If the only problem is the person you report to, think about all other aspects of the job before deciding whether to pack it in. Can you rise above this? Develop your inner resources to help cultivate a thicker skin? Ask yourself: 'What can I learn from this?' The Tao teaches that no one can hurt you when you have found your highest path.

CASE STUDY

Sally was a marketing manager in her late twenties who came to me because her boss's grand-standing actions at her expense made her feel invisible. He fronted all of her work and she got no recognition for it, though she did get a huge salary. When she came to see me she was frustrated, angry and busy fantasising about resigning. However, everything else about the job was great so this was a drastic step. The first thing she had to get clear about was that she was unfulfilled due to her own attachment to getting the recognition she thought she deserved. Fulfilment must come from within. She couldn't see the tremendous brilliance of what she already achieved and did.

Because her boss did not value her she allowed this to affect her and make her incapable of valuing herself. It was his problem; he didn't show her appreciation. She realised that although she played a role in his success, she was not irreplaceable. Be realistic! Remember the thousand of eager graduate trainees dying for your job! She wanted to keep hers so I suggested she keeps a non-attachment to her perceived 'profile' in her company and find her personal value in a job well done. She missed one major point: You don't work for your boss. You work for yourself. None of your employers or colleagues is going to be perfect, but your job is to give your best.

In this case, as in many, it was a simple situation of two individuals not seeing eye to eye; two people with different strengths and limitations in the way they communicate. Although you cannot change your boss's management style you can adapt your response to him. Experts call this 'managing up' as opposed to just expecting to be managed. You could be kinder about the flaws in your boss's approach and try to be more supportive towards him even if your values are polarised.

REFLECT

Buddhist philosophy asserts that outward conflicts between people are almost always a product of inner conflicts within those people. Message: resolve your internal conflict about prestige and recognition and recapture your original enthusiasm for your work.

OBSTACLE 3:
"THE CORPORATE CULTURE AT MY FIRM IS ALL WRONG."

We have seen in earlier chapters the types of attitudes and issues in the workplace that put employees off and an arrogant, bullying leader is one of the worst scenarios. Business leaders have a choice: they can build bridges or create barriers with their staff. Talking down to them will just create tension and cause resentment to build up. A healthy company needs empowered and benevolent workers and leaders. This ripples into happy customers and greater profits.

CASE STUDY

Fiona worked for a small publishing company. It was run by a man staff referred to behind his back as 'the dinosaur'. This chairman had started the company himself 25 years ago and though it was still successful, it was nowhere near its potential. Everyone, but 'the dinosaur' could see it. This was because this man was set in his ways and would not allow the many talented people beneath him to shine. Over the years this attitude had permeated its way down through the company into a culture of bosses caring more about their own entrenched positions than helping their staff develop.

No one below board level had any authority; the tiniest things had to be signed off by the powers that be. Fiona was a junior business manager in charge of a group of specialist magazines. She had been at the company only a year and was getting increasingly disillusioned. She thought she had done her research properly before joining the company, but it hadn't included talking to anyone who actually worked there. At her previous firm, Fiona had enjoyed a great deal of autonomy and the freedom to develop projects of her choice and bring them to fruition. Here, her creativity was completely stymied.

Fiona was incredibly frustrated when she came to see me, but we quickly worked out that her situation was very simple. She would have no trouble finding a position more in line with her expectations at a different company. Her level of dissatisfaction meant that unless things changed in her present company, that was the best option. She talked this over with her immediate superior, who felt just as she did about 'the dinosaur'. He made an appointment to see this man and outline some of their ideas for making their department more efficient. The result was that this man was told off for speaking out of turn and shouted out of the chairman's office.

Fiona now wrote a letter to this chairman, telling him that she sadly felt her position to be untenable. However, she left the door open for negotiations should he wish to go down this road. He didn't. She was called by the human resources department the same day and told that she should leave immediately. Although she'd be paid for her notice period they did not wish her to work it. Fiona quickly found a better position at a progressive company and does not regret her decision to take charge of her fate. Sadly, not every company is going to become a great place to work. The trick is in recognising what you can change and what you cannot. You can change your attitude or change your job. You can't change the ogre.

REFLECT

The spiritual forum is a valuable commodity – and it's free! They are popping up in more and more forward-thinking companies. They are not about universal agreement on everything, but about a meeting of different mindsets. It's good to listen to others talking about the spiritual issues that affect them. Who could you approach in your company to suggest this idea?

The Breakthrough

*"You can't solve a problem on
the same level that created it."*

ALBERT EINSTEIN, PHYSICIST & NOBLE PRIZE WINNER

Renewal and regeneration happen every day. Each day is new, a chance to change our life if we wish. Each moment is a chance to do something differently. In his seminars, motivational speaker Tony Robbins often reminds audiences that once they make the decision, they can transform their lives 'in a heartbeat'.

Now that you have read through the previous few pages are you any clearer about where you need to go from here? In a nutshell, your decisions will fall into one of two broad categories. It's more likely than not that you will be able to transform your experience within your current job. However, some of you, while reading this book, will have felt a growing sense that you need to leave your current job, company or profession. And I know from experience that quite a few of you are now just plain confused; uncertain about what you should do with this knowledge.

Once again, the path to peace is the following: *change what you can't accept then accept what you can't change.* To do otherwise is to leave yourself in a state of frustration and resentment which will prevent you from being your best. To stay clear and fresh, rivers must keep moving. So must you. Serious introspection and profound change can come without a whiff of crisis. That is wisdom at its best.

After all, there is nothing in the definition of change that necessitates disharmony. Think of this as an opportunity for personal growth and for fine-tuning aspects of your life that you may have neglected to your detriment. Different periods of life focus one's energy differently.

Is it logical to stay in a job you hate? Probably not. There are no medals for spending a lifetime doing something you hate. But that doesn't mean there is an *immediate* answer to the next question: "What am I supposed to do now then?" It is easy to fall prey to fear of the unknown. Perhaps what you are supposed to be doing just now is *not knowing* what you are meant to be doing just now. Step away from the egotism of presuming that you should know. Turning down a road with no map can be anxiety-producing and exhilarating at the same time. Our footing is less certain, but look at the expanded views.

If you are confused about what you love doing, maybe you stopped listening to yourself a long time ago. Try this: let go of doing habitual things for a day or two – away from your routine. You will start to see things more clearly and notice what you are noticing. Next time a little voice says, 'This is exciting', LISTEN. Go to the library and notice what grabs you on the shelves. Try new things. Give yourself some time and space to be by yourself. You are not likely to find your life direction while slumped in front of the television.

See an undefined future as an opportunity rather than a problem. Think: "I'm so lucky to be entering a phase of my life in which I don't need answers." When we put aside reasoning, we make some of our greatest discoveries. Electricity was not discovered using reasoning and neither were polio vaccines. Just start experimenting. There's no reason to let the arbitrary 'barriers' of age or stage of life stop you from doing whatever is in your heart. I know a woman who graduated at age 82.

Have you noticed how we seek security, but as soon as we have it we risk it. Watch a toddler look around to check his mother is there and then venture further away. It is the promise of new discoveries that drives us. We try to balance our lives between the comfort of security and the excitement of new experiences.

Shifting is a gradual and continuous process and that never stops. You have to be continually devoted through whatever practice works for you. Remember also, that doing what you love is not a sure fire guarantee for an easier life. It is a recipe for a fulfilling, meaningful life where you are likely to embrace more responsibilities.

We create our limitations, we must destroy them. We say things like, "I can't reach that dream, I need money to start that business" or "What's the point, I am only ever going to be an accountant because this job pays the bills". We often love our issues, our problems and want to keep them. They form our identity – what would we be without our problems eh?

What would you do with your life if you had no problems? Please think deeply about this. If you look carefully at the structure of your mind, you will see that you take great meaning from solving your problems. But instead of solving them and being grateful we must create another problem! If it is not real, you will create one or go out and borrow someone else's! I would challenge you to try living the next month believing you had no problems. Watch your resistance.

REFLECT

THE RIVER NAMED YOU

Think of the course of your career or business as a river. Chart where you faced big decisions and changed course. Note where you had the most turbulence and how you got to calmer waters. Mark significant milestones and places where you found a dead end – where you stopped for fun. Any amazing waterfalls?

Where is your source and what are the important in-flows into your business?

Notice if the river is shallow, vast, in a mountainous region or does it run through a city?

What is your ultimate destination – is it the sea?

Be creative with this one and enjoy. Take your time. This is a discovery process. Not a board report.

A Richer Life

*"If you choose to use your status and influence
to raise your voice on behalf of those who
have no voice; if you choose to identify not
only with the powerful, but with the powerless;
if you retain the ability to imagine yourself
into the lives of those who do not have your
advantages, then it will not only be your proud
families who celebrate your existence, but
thousands and millions of people whose reality
you have helped change. We do not need magic
to change the world, we carry all the power
we need inside ourselves already: we have
the power to imagine better."*

**JK ROWLING'S (AUTHOR OF HARRY POTTER)
SPEECH TO 2008 HARVARD GRADUATES**

As you lie in your bed at night, what tugs at your
heartstrings? Opportunity knocks not only once, but
constantly until we answer the call. Often we ignore it or
are afraid to answer. The choice is yours. Only when you
become tired of needless suffering will you take the steps
to move beyond it. Have you had enough yet? Why wait
for the next nervous breakdown, redundancy, divorce or
heart attack to change the situation?

One of the most striking insights I have had is that when we
spend our time doing things like worrying, arguing our

points, procrastinating or mindless consumption – we are giving away our *life energy* which we have a limited supply of. Ask yourself the next time you feel fear or anxiety brewing up inside – is this worth x hours of my life energy? Your view of your life will change. Get rid of phrases like 'I should', 'I ought' and 'there was no choice' from you vernacular. Guilt has no place in the power of personal choice. These thoughts create unnecessary pressure.

> *"The cost of a thing is the amount of life which is required to be exchanged for it, immediately or in the long run."*
>
> **HENRY DAVID THOREAU**

The simpler life with deeper meaning, more time for loved ones, less attachment to status symbols is not for everyone, but its appeal is growing because it improves quality of life. Why? Because it is in line with natural principles. You don't have to lower your standard of living. You will find you have enormous vitality because your time is spent working at things you enjoy and because you have created an environment you are best suited to. You won't get bored or tired because there is harmony in your character and your choice of work.

Imagine getting up in the morning and looking forward to the day ahead. A less cluttered, less consumer-driven life will help you thrive on this path to freedom and financial independence. Don't fall into the trap of believing your self-worth and psychological security comes from your job title and what you earn. That is society's conditioning and you don't need to swallow the bait. Our belief that 'more is better' is not fulfilling. When you are taking your last few breaths will you really be thinking of the properties you did or did not buy at the right time? My work with hospice cancer patients certainly puts it all into context. The biggest regrets that they share with me are not doing things that they really wanted to do and not spending enough time with the people that really matter.

If we want to enjoy work environments that support and sustain life we must begin by recognising that where life resides is in the heart. You are at the perfect place to use your head and heart to elevate yourself and your business. The very fact that you have chosen to read this book is a sign that you are ready for new possibilities that can change your experience of the workplace forever.

A life of purpose is built step by step. Start your journey. Set small goals and go for them. They will immediately make you feel better. Once you have decided, make a commitment to stick to your decision. This will only happen if you develop the habit of personal integrity and this is simply keeping your personal promises.

Alice: Would you tell me, please,
which way I ought to go from here?

Cat: That depends a good deal
on where you want to get to.

Alice: I don't much care where.

Cat: Then it doesn't matter which way you go.

FROM 'ALICE IN WONDERLAND' BY LEWIS CARROLL

Your awakening is a gradual shift and you might notice the trademarks of a business head and spiritual heart manifesting in your life: a spontaneous generosity of spirit, a willingness to embrace spiritual principles in your work, and a transformation whereby you are no longer driven by fear and acquisition. It will seem natural and easier to access flow while remaining fully engaged in all the events unfolding around you.

Glow from the inside, play vigorously to taste the joy of living that is your birthright – but don't play only to win. Do not underestimate what you do when you work and play. Your mindset is very significant and contributes not only to your well-being but to our amazing world.

Even what you do in the next minute and the spirit in which you do it can make a huge difference. Our richness lies in the lives we have touched and the way in which we make a difference during our time on this planet. As Mahatma Gandhi wisely advised: *"Be the change you want to see in the world"*.

Many lives are run on default. What will be the shock or unknown event that jolts you out of automatic pilot? Give yourself the chance to reflect and to embrace those long lost dreams and aspirations by making time to consciously evaluate your strengths, habits and needs and define clearly what you want and will be happiest doing.

Randy Crawford sings that hauntingly beautiful song: *"One day I'll fly away…"* How can you make your 'one day' happen now?

REFLECT

IMAGINE YOUR PERFECT WORKING DAY

What happens the moment you arrive at your office? Where is your office? Imagine your staff and your clients – the quality of your conversations with them.

Hear yourself speaking with passion and integrity. What kind of services or products does your business sell? Picture every detail.

Now ask yourself what you can do before this evening ends to experience an element of that perfect working day, from the emotions you feel to the interactions. How can you initiate great client networks when your rolodex is almost empty? Discover the element of your dream that are symbols of what you most love and value. You can bring them into your life right now, wherever you are, whatever you are doing. Perhaps your perfect workplace is by the sea – keep shells on your desk to start the manifestation process and set your intent.

"Do. Or do not. There is no try."

YODA, JEDI MASTER, STAR WARS

Don't Let A Good 'Credit Crunch' Crisis Go To Waste

"But as the economy contracts, we must resist our natural reflex to contract with it. Instead, we need to do the opposite. Expansion is the best way to survive any crisis… Fear deprives people of choice. Fear shrinks the world into isolated, defensive enclaves. Fear spirals out of control. Fear makes everyday life seem clouded over with danger."

DEEPAK CHOPRA, MD (PIONEER OF ALTERNATIVE MEDICINE)
IN THE SAN FRANCISCO CHRONICLE NEWSPAPER (NOVEMBER 19TH 2008)

Only a fool would glamorise recession or claim it is good for us. It hurts… it has the voracity to plunge our lives into chaos as we carry around feelings of mounting insecurity. The good things in life such as our homes and sending our children to private school now appear to us as hefty burdens. How quickly perceptions shift in times of uncertainty. Sudden change disorientates us and as our old reality disappears we stay stuck for a while in transit refusing to let go rather than discover our new reality.

Life has a way of bringing you back to places you thought you had left behind. I was made redundant from a job that I loved and was hugely committed to. The corporate machinery spat out whole departments without mercy. A brutal jolt that leaves you in no doubt of how expendable you are when it comes to ensuring partner profits do not drop at all costs. One could say that you have to be naive to believe partner profits are not a priority in a commercial organisation. It would be a rare find indeed for board members to valiantly choose to save the livelihoods of loyal staff as opposed to succumbing to the grasping greed that this sort of terminal action really amounts to. Yet we do see from time to time this sort of integrity and benevolence that people do not forget.

For a while, I felt vulnerable and angry to be pushed out of work in the worst economic recession known in history. Yet I left with good grace fulfilling my duty to my employer until the last day with a smile. Not only had a big chunk of my life gone, with the spell broken every aspect of my life seemed to be filled with disenchantment. Life looked so different I hardly recognised it. Change broke up my old identity just as it did when I was divorced a decade ago and moved back to London from Vancouver. It felt like déjà vu – this strange inner emptiness that revisited me after all these years. Nothing seemed solid – everything was up for grabs and I had no idea what would come next, so anything was possible. Scary.

Decay and destruction are built into nature and each of us lives in a world that is meant to dry up in its time like a withering flower to make way for new growth that follows. Competent managers resign, clients are enticed by our competitors, suppliers go bankrupt. We panic and try to fix things mechanistically oblivious that these problematic situations indicate an imminent transition.

Acceptance requires time and a humble heart. I remembered how after my divorce I took some time out, walked for miles to the sites of beautiful Renaissance Tuscan monasteries, and sat beside many deep wells. I could appreciate now first hand why people in transition frequently visit sacred pilgrimage sites. I found the courage to let go after spending time doing nothing but listening and watching life. I left with a feeling of deep peace, reverence for the majesty of the universe and a renewed sense of purpose with ideas that began to take shape in the months to come.

Whatever its form, spiritual presence or power stuns the curious mind with its soothing healing, its kinship with nature. I could see how personal crisis can open up spiritual vistas if we can stay grounded and stop catastrophising our situation, making it sound like the worst thing ever, even though it may seem that way. There will be the age-old tranquil caterpillar to butterfly rebirth part to the experience if we stay calm and as detached as possible from the external unfolding drama. Change is part of life's curriculum.

Change is also something we naturally resist. Fear of the unknown can be so overwhelming that we can stay stuck in the same position for years. Often we stick to draining situations rather than venture into unfamiliar territory. What we don't notice is that in between the letting go and the getting a grip again of life, there is a chaotic but potentially creative period where things aren't the old way, but aren't really a new way yet either. This time is precious – it is where we re-design ourselves and give birth to a new possibility. It is not the time to start feeling a profound failure. Now is not the time to believe nothing good will ever happen to you again and that you will never recover from this. Of course we are all vulnerable to experiences in which our sense of personal worth or adequacy is challenged. When we are mentally weakened by our fears we tend to recall old hurts and an insurmountable feeling of loss of control.

Yet many people can turn this into a developmental transition where they realise there are alternatives to what is happening to them. In aboriginal culture they have a ceremony to honour this 'wilderness' period where the youth goes on a vision quest walk as a rite of passage. In modern society we do not even have a name for this zone and in any case we are in too much of a hurry to consider its special meaning for us. In symbolic terms, I see this as a rich, fertile place, which we can embrace with fasting, prayers, cleansing rituals, pilgrimage or giving to charity. This expansive behaviour liberates us from the fear of the unknown. In this state of mind we will be wired to receive guidance and fresh insights that will help us move forward with a strong backbone. Feelings of loss begin to subside and something new will emerge. This is the way of transformation. This is the bountiful state of grace.

Today, we are aware life is changing faster than it ever has before. The challenge that faces the world is to learn and do things differently. Whilst economic rescue plans are announced, emotional strains are taking their toll on marriages and hardships abound. Raymond, a banker friend of mine lost his job and he and his wife no longer eat out, grow their own vegetables in a local allotment nor plan holidays. The priority is to keep his daughter at private school. "We've stopped everything," he said. "We're going back to how we used to live as students with very little money. I am just too tired and worried about the future to enjoy being with the family."

Many of us have felt instinctively that our crazy credit-dependent lifestyles could not continue forever. The country thought itself rich. The events that have brought this recession had already started long before we admitted it to ourselves, long before we even noticed. In 1720 Jonathan Swift, author of *Gulliver's Travels*, said of the bursting of the South Sea Bubble: *"Men thought it would come, but no one was prepared for it - it came like a thief in the night."*

With the shock comes focus on new things. The lesson seemed clear – the method of incentivising bankers was deeply flawed. It bred a mercenary, individualistic approach that threw away collective ownership, professional ethics and long-term loyalty. The players were motivated purely by money and less by loyalty to the company, and were highly enticed by huge bonuses. Now as swathes of professionals face redundancy, companies are replacing the implicit contract of mutual responsibility with a blatant sense of the expendability of people. This is fear-based decision making.

Here's the paradox, it is even more important now for companies to remember that they are only as good as their people, so training and recruitment of talent must be a priority. This is expansive thinking and not the knee-jerk reactions that we are seeing in the city where massive culling is the order of the day.

So, the idea of being spiritual at work might sound a bit contradictory; impossible even, especially in a downturn. We're all meant to be competing and making cost efficiencies, aren't we? How do we do this compassionately? It's not like 'loving' the staff will win you market share, will it? Yet that is exactly what turned SW Airlines round at a difficult time. They hit a crisis and they needed to do something drastic to cut costs. Instead of laying people off their MD sold some expensive planes. His intention was pure and clear: there was no way he was going to hurt his people so, as far as he was concerned, cutting staff was not an option. Now, from a business point of view, this sounded very noble… but possibly untenable. But this leader generated such a wave of loyalty, respect and motivation in his people that they literally dragged the company out of trouble, straight back into impressive profitability. It is a fantastic example of conscious spiritual leadership – and the amazing energy it can unleash.

This man recognised the value of his loyal staff and made a commitment to support them and by doing so he laid himself on the line for them. He made a decision that defied reason. It was unusual, brave, and quite emotional… And the staff at SW Airlines were very emotional in the way they responded: they gave everything they had to get the business back on track. Because they did not just work for the company any more; they were the company.

How many CEOs only look out for themselves when the ship is sinking? We have seen many examples of key figures in the financial sector fiercely securing their unbelievably massive pension pot above all else, including shareholders.

You might think the judgment of the MD at SW Airline was a little unsound; a bit rash maybe. However, there is a spiritual dimension to leadership that goes beyond normal logic. Sure, you have to be a competent manager but if you can also use your emotional intelligence - your intuition -

you get to expand your options… and a whole world of possibility opens up for you and it benefits everyone.

One of the spiritual benefits, if we seize it, that we can gain during an economic recession is that as we tighten our budgets and we change our lifestyle, we can actually begin getting a clearer picture of what we actually need. We may be surprised to find that we need very little as we simplify our affairs.

The Government would like us to spend ourselves out of this fiasco, but the public have wised up to the fact that just because something is expensive it doesn't make it necessary. Comfort shopping has left our homes crammed with meaningless rubbish. We could find more return on our investments in our gardens than the stock exchange as seeds grow into organic healthy vegetables. We may take up walking and find new inspiration from our surroundings, stemming the growing obesity threat. Fresh perspectives blossom if we choose differently this time.

Ironically in an age of austerity we are still the privileged ones who can choose to drink and smoke less and lay off rich food that clog our arteries with fat. Many of us are now spending more time with the family enjoying board games and reading books again. You may have sadly noticed the boarded up shops and the despondency on faces in trains and bus stations. Yet you can also find that there is a new togetherness amongst the ordinary people even if it is against the bankers and politicians!

Unprecedented tragedies such as the Tsunami, September 11th Terrorist attack and the collapse of the world economy with traditional financial structures falling apart, are active cues. These stark, destructive, mammoth blows are macro metaphors for an inner ending that it is time to make. Just as redundancy, divorce, death – outer losses - are micro metaphors for some inner relinquishment that must be made.

It is no more enlightening to passively invoke karma as a reason for our 'punishments' or to ask 'why is this happening to me?' When we encounter these poignant signals in our lives we can move forward more effectively if we ask ourselves what it is time to let go of? It could be qualities such as selfishness, greed, hatred or ignorance. It could be an addiction to change to escape from the real issues raised in your life such as moving on from one relationship to another but taking along with you the same old attitude that destroyed your marriages. Walking away from our deeply held beliefs is one of the hardest things to do and we often use any means to justify keeping them. Without them the world can seem strange and frightening. No wonder we are reluctant.

What learnings can we take from all these events that will help us grow individually as people as well as a world? An important lesson here is one of safety, comfort, security – and one of complacency. It is interesting how so many of us feel an inherent almost tangible feeling of safety working in 'blue chip' organisations and living in a modern western country. We are lulled into a false sense of comfort which allows us to take so much for granted. It is as if we are invincible and expect to be divinely shielded from atrocities that only poorer nations can continually bear. As if we have a superior first class birthright in the worldly scheme of things. That living under the umbrella of the American or British flag or the glamour of a corporate giant such as Lehman Brothers will guarantee us not only material prosperity but also personal comfort and safety.

This feeling is not really misplaced as in many ways the West achieves standards of excellence that are unsurpassed anywhere else in the world. Yet it is only by the grace of a higher force that each of the billions of neurons in our brain continue to function properly, allowing us to breathe. No insurance policy could have protected those poor people washed away by the Tsunami or working in the twin towers on that fateful day. The tragedy struck the top CEOs as brutally as it did the cleaning staff. Death swooped on those with Harvard PhDs as it did on those who dropped out of high school. It struck those living in the affluent suburbs of Long Island as it struck those sharing cramped apartments in Soho. So let us be grateful for all our blessings - for we have many in the western world.

So how can we start to expand instead of contract in these difficult times of fear and insecurity?

While the economy is falling far short today, perhaps a trillion dollars or more short, we should never lose sight of its potential. We have the most productive workers in the world, the greatest universities and capacity for innovation, an incredible amount of resilience, entrepreneurship and flexibility, and the most diverse and creative population of any major economy. We have a lot to offer and can create businesses that think in new, innovative and spiritual ways.

We are capable of rescuing ourselves by changing our way of relating to each other and our business. The holographic principle is an invitation to see the world as deeply interconnected. When an issue arises in our business, we tend to look at it as if through a microscope - what exactly is going on with this issue? This can be helpful. We can, however, also choose to look at it from a 'macroscopic' perspective. How is this problem a reflection of bigger problems in the business? How might these in turn be connected to wider issues in society and in the world? This will give us far greater perspectives. It means that as I solve 'my' problem it will have an impact on the rest of the company, and in some small yet significant way, even on the world. For example, part of my corporate social responsibility programme is the decision to switch off the lights in the office when not needed. This saves the business money as well as saves precious energy and reduces the company's carbon footprint on the earth.

If businesses embrace a willingness to see and think holographically we might expect to see an emphasis also on resolving conflicts and dealing with issues rather than letting them fester. So I might choose to move beyond scapegoats and focus on understanding how each role in my company really works and the degree of contribution at every level. It gives me an insight into trends appearing and how they might reflect world issues. For instance, diversity issues and the impact of cultural awareness improvements that might be required.

I was working with a large multinational a few years ago and I noticed brittle tension between a key manager and Joe the director who had instructed my consultancy firm. Accountability and commitment levels in that team were low. All felt the friction between the two but it was the white elephant in the room and acknowledged by none. Working my way into this was not easy, but after building trust I gently probed into this and both agreed there was an issue between them. We contracted a session after work to facilitate an honest discussion so they had a chance to air their feelings. This released pent up grievances and after some further coaching it led to a much easier working relationship and the energy was unblocked and started to flow better, which resulted in the team securing two key accounts.

Remember staff are likely to be feeling insecure, nervous and stressed at this time and may manifest difficult behaviours in the workplace. Often when one key relationship is blocked the whole project could be similarly blocked and by wisely targeting the effective point you are address the underlying problem. Look at the issue as both personal and systemic. If you set your intention to help release tensions and fears in your people with an understanding and loving heart they will respond well. Reassure wherever you can that you are on their side and you have every faith in them to succeed. Now is the time to affirm this positively and sincerely and you will see your profits rise even in a downturn.

What if we acted in ways that acknowledge and embrace the presence of something beyond the physical here and now, beyond that which we perceive with our senses? In a business where this dimension of spirituality is thriving we might see a willingness and calmness to live in the realm of uncertainty in the place of the known and expected. Where managers have an inner confidence of being able to ride out the recession and honour their intuition and hunches in favour of rule-governed behaviour where everything is justified in terms of pre-set criteria. So new ideas are welcomed and where they can admit they 'don't know' instead of fearing for their jobs if they appear not to have all the answers. We might see businesses that are comfortable with metaphors that look to nature as a teacher and that pay attention to natural and seasonal rhythms. For example, planning more internal work on purpose and vision in the winter months where days are short and a good time for introspection. Then preparing for more goal-related activity in Spring and Summer. We could enjoy the presence of mystery and see things unfold in a natural rhythm.

Now is the time to think not of money but of value. Stay close to your clients. Remember they are also likely to be affected by the economic storm and this is a time to listen sympathetically to them. Be reassuring and help them understand recessions are a natural cyclical phase of a healthy economy and that all recessions end. Seek to contribute and take attention away from yourself in ways that add value to your clients. For instance, you could run free of charge morning or lunchtime training around critical issues that currently affect them.

Be understanding of clients who may be showing signs of inertia – they too are worried of spending right now. They might want time to think about your proposals. Bullying or high-pressure sales techniques are not going to endear or create long-term bonds with your paymasters. Create a positive space with your clients. Suggest going for a walk in the park with your client or having coffee in a relaxing bar together to explore ideas and collaborate. Simply listening to them will bring closeness and develop a trusting relationship. It's not about making unrealistic promises to them but rather using a combination of your expertise and knowledge of their business to create aspirational outcomes for them even if it is in the longer term. It may take a little longer to close a sale – the client may be much more demanding and you may have to repeatedly prove your value with supporting evidence for your pitch. But when you succeed, you don't just sell your product or services – you sell hope which counters fear. 'Business as usual' feels wonderful on many levels when it happens at a time when the odds are against such buoyant activity.

Many people are focussing so much energy on things like unemployment insurance, scrimping and holding back. But don't put the majority of your efforts there – start looking forward for new opportunities and network amongst like-minded entrepreneurs. Seek out places and people that are succeeding during the current recession. I promise you will find them. If you are made redundant look at other exciting industries where they are still recruiting and actively seek vibrant forward thinking companies who believe in their people. Show your flexibility and remember to highlight your transferable skills.

We have control over the meaning we give to circumstances. I know I have a choice in the perspective which I use to interpret this time in our history. I refuse to let the media or Government tell me how to live my life and allow them to paint their picture of my reality – one of hopeless doom and gloom. This time of adversity is not the darkness of loss, but is as they say in children's stories where you find *the treasure*. A colossal opportunity if ever, to finally change your life and live it in a way that nourishes your soul everyday, every moment.

REFLECT

See if you can find the 'gift' in the perceived adversity. Ask yourself:

- How can I use this adversity to become a better person?
- How can I use this opportunity to serve others?
- What can I do to shift into a more resourceful state?

About The Author

Shilpa Unalkat, LL.B, DHP (MNRHP)

Shilpa is recognised as a world-class facilitator of conscious leadership skills. She works closely with aspiring entrepreneurs and International organisations that actively follow the conscious business philosophy. They are aware of the effects of their actions and act in ways that consciously affect human beings and the environment in a beneficial way. They follow principles of doing no harm and the triple bottom line model of providing positive value in the domain of people, planet and profit. They desire to benefit not only the external livelihood but also the internal lives of their employees who enjoy a wellness affirming workplace.

As a former city lawyer working in a magic circle law firm, Shilpa understands the pressures facing professionals in the corporate world. By teaching a combination of leadership skills and personal mastery techniques, she works to release her clients' desire for authenticity and personal power. The underlying philosophy is that the concept of total responsibility for one's life and the wisdom to grow from difficult challenges turns people's lives around. That every stage or transition in our lives can be a step toward our own more authentic presence in the world.

Shilpa grew up in a very loving, Hindu Gujarati family who arrived in the UK, when she was a toddler, just before Idi Amin's brutal Ugandan exodus in 1972. She has always been deeply inspired by her parents' grace and grit attitude. They showed great resilience in the face of a life-changing ordeal. They endured having their ancestral home, business and all worldly possessions snatched away by a dictator, forcing them to start all over again in a foreign land. Shilpa is highly influenced by their entrepreneurial spirit and inner faith that far from something to fear, change - even the most painful - gives us many opportunities. That adversity does not mean defeat. That a loss in worldly terms can often lead to spiritual success. They gently instilled in her the belief that by being both ambitious and spiritual, a person could achieve their heart's desires with the blessings of a higher force.

These familial 'gifts' gave her an unquestionable sense of inner security and a metaphysical perspective on life that reassures of an ever-unfolding good that stands as the natural order of the universe. From childhood she was aware of the bridge between the inner and outer worlds through powerful ceremonial Hindu rituals, prayers, meditation and forms of yoga. The idea that the universe responds to us on many levels if we are ready to listen continues to be the basis of her psychological way of being. It permeates and informs her style of working as a success coach and trainer.

Shilpa can be contacted on shilpa@shilpaunalkat.com or by calling 07876 444 111.

Website: www.shilpaunalkat.com

References

Tom Peters *In Search Of Excellence: Lessons From America's Best-Run Companies,* Harper Business, 0060150424

Mihaly Csikszentmihalyi, *Finding Flow,* Basic Books, 0465024114

Eckhart Tolle, *The Power Of Now,* Mobius, 0340733500

Alain de Botton, *Status Anxiety,* Penguin, 0141014865

Robert Kiyosaki, *Rich Dad, Poor Dad: What The Rich Teach Their Kids About Money That The Poor And Middle Class Do Not,* Time Warner, 0751532711

Global Equity Strategy, *It Doesn't Pay: Materialism And The Pursuit Of Happiness,* Dresdner Kleinwort Wasserstein, 3 November 2005

The Foundation for Inner Peace, *A Course In Miracles.* Arkana, USA, 1997

Oprah Winfrey, *O, The Oprah Magazine,* September 2001 Edition

Charles Handy, *The Age Of Paradox,* Harvard Business School Press, 0875844251

Joe Tye, *Staying On Top: When The World's Upside Down,* Paradox 21 Press

Elizabeth Debold, *What Is Enlightenment* magazine. Article entitled 'The Business Of Saving The World' in the March 2005 issue

Alfie Kohn, *No contest: The Case Against Competition,* Houghton Mifflin, 0395631254

Richard Barrett, *Liberating the Corporate Soul,* Butterworth-Heinemann, 0750670711

James C. Collins & Jerry I. Porras, *Built To Last: Successful Habits of Visionary Companies,* Harper Collins, 0887307396

Manfred Kets de Vries, Article entitled *High Anxiety.* The Guardian on 17 September 2005

Ken Blanchard, Bill Hybels, Phil Hodges, *Leadership by the Book: Tools To Transform Your Workplace,* Harper Collins, 0007114532

'The Business Of Saving The World' by Elizabeth Debold in the March 2005 issue of *What Is Enlightenment* magazine

Featured Organisations

Timberland – *www.timberland.com*

Plug Power – *www.plugpower.com*

HSBC – *www.hsbc.co.uk*

Grameen Bank – *www.grameen-info.org*

Covey Leadership Centre – *www.franklincovey.com*

The Body Shop – *www.thebodyshop.co.uk*

Microsoft – *www.microsoft.com*

ANZ Bank – *www.anz.com*

People Tree – *www.peopletree.co.uk*

Divine Chocolate – *www.divinechocolate.com*

Vodaphone – *www.vodaphone.co.uk*

Whole Foods – *www.wholefoodsmarket.com*

Interra Project – *www.interraproject.org*

Generon Consulting – *www.generonconsulting.com*

Brahma Kumaris – *www.bkwsu.org*

A FEELING OF
WORTH

A Manifesto For Mending Our Broken World

BAY JORDAN

www.leanmarketingpress.com

Persuasion Skills

BLACK BOOK

Practical NLP Language Patterns for
Getting The Response You Want

Rintu Basu

FREE INSIDE
'Black Book'
Persuasion
Training
E-course

www.ingramcontent.com/pod-product-compliance
Lightning Source LLC
Chambersburg PA
CBHW070914270326
41927CB00011B/2566